the SuperJam cookbook

the
Super Jam
Cookbook

Over 75 recipes,
from jams to jammy dodgers
and marmalades to muffins

Fraser Doherty

EBURY
PRESS

1 3 5 7 9 10 8 6 4 2

Published in 2010 by Ebury Press, an im

A Random House Group Company

Text copyright © Fraser Doherty 2010
Photography copyright © Ebury Press 20

The Random House Group Limited Reg. No. 954009

Addresses for companies within the Random House Group can
be found at www.randomhouse.co.uk

A CIP catalogue record for this book is available from the British Library

The Random House Group Limited supports The Forest Stewardship
Council (FSC), the leading international forest certification organisation.
All our titles that are printed on Greenpeace approved FSC certified
paper carry the FSC logo. Our paper procurement policy can be found
at www.rbooks.co.uk/environment

To buy books by your favourite authors and register for offers visit
www.rbooks.co.uk

Design: Smith & Gilmour
Photography: Noel Murphy
Food styling: Marie-Ange Lapierre
Prop styling: Tessa Evelegh

Printed and bound in China by C&C Offset Printing Co. Ltd

ISBN 9780091936143 (paperback)
ISBN 9780091938642 (hardback)

contents

jams 27

marmalades 51

jellies 61

curds 67

chutneys 75

special spreads 85

jammy treats 101

This book is dedicated to my grandmother, Susan Doherty. My entire career in jam has been inspired by my gran as without her teaching me to make it I'd never have done any of this. Nan, thank you for sharing your jam-making secrets with me!

the story of SuperJam

(A bit of blah blah before we get stuck in)

I've always loved jam. As a kid I liked nothing better than a big dollop of my Irish grandmother Susan's jam on well-buttered crusty bread. My gran makes the best jam. She's perfected her recipes over the course of her life and luckily, one afternoon when I was fourteen, she shared her jam-making secrets with me.

The process fascinated me and watching her was really exciting. The same day, I ran round to the supermarket and bought a bag of sugar and some fruit. I made a few pots of my own jam and was so proud of it; it tasted almost as good as my gran's. Before it had even cooled down I handed the pots out to the neighbours to see what they thought. Thankfully, they were as enthusiastic about my jam as I was. Within a few days, I had to make more; and this time they paid me one pound fifty for each jar. I was soon knocking on doors all over the neighbourhood and everyone thought my jam was wonderful. I came up with loads of recipes for jams, marmalades and curds and started selling them at church fêtes, farmers' markets and to local delicatessens.

At sixteen, I left school so that I could make jam every day. It seemed like a perfect career choice. But after about six months the business had grown so large that I couldn't make enough jam in my

parents' tiny little kitchen any more. I was going to have to come up with a 'big idea' in order to be able to move into a factory.

I wanted to transform the world of jam for ever. Because jam can be so unhealthy and has a bit of an old-fashioned image, sales have been in decline for decades. I was really terrified by the idea of jam becoming extinct.

I set myself the goal of coming up with a healthier way to make jam. It took hundreds of attempts. I eventually worked out how to make jam entirely from fruit and fruit juice, without adding any sugar or anything artificial. To make it as healthy as possible, I used 'superfruits', like blueberries and cranberries, which are said to be very good for you. That was the birth of 'SuperJam'.

The products are now sold in supermarkets all over Europe, including most of the big ones in this country. I get asked to speak about my story all over the world, have won about twenty awards and even one day had dinner with Gordon Brown at Downing Street (ooh, get you). All that from a kid who left school at sixteen so that he could make jam every day!

the SuperJam
tea parties

(A pot of tea, a laugh and some dancing)

My gran would make jam, scones and cakes and take them round to all the lonely elderly people in her area. These were people who were living alone or in care homes; nobody else visited them very much and, in some ways, nobody else cared about them. It was something that my gran felt, and still does feel, very strongly about, and every time we went to see her she would drag my brother and me with her to visit the elderly people. While she would make lunch for them, my brother would play his guitar and I would tell them stories of how I wanted to set up my own business one day. One particular lady, Mary, would joke that I was going to get into 'monkey business', having forgotten she had made the same joke every time we had visited her over the years.

As kids we didn't really understand the boredom that some of these people faced, and couldn't quite appreciate why they would cry when we left. We were pretty young at the time, but we knew there was something sad about them having the exact same conversation with us every time we visited, since they could barely remember anything for longer than a few minutes.

As I got older, and once the business had taken off, I found myself in a position where I could do something about the problem of elderly people being lonely, since it had become something that

I, too, felt strongly about – rates of suicide are alarmingly high among women over the age of seventy, and over a million elderly people in this country spend Christmas Day on their own.

By no means was I going to come up with the solution to this massive problem, but as I began speaking with local councillors and community groups it became clear that the biggest thing lacking in many elderly people's lives was the opportunity to socialise outside their own house or care home.

So in April 2007, SuperJam started running tea parties in local community halls in my home town of Edinburgh. We would have live music, dancing, pots of tea and, of course, scones and SuperJam. It was a very simple concept but it quickly flourished. A year later, we had run over a hundred events in Scotland, England and Wales, with the biggest events attracting over five hundred guests!

A lot of the guests wanted to contribute to the project, by bringing along home baking or knitting tea cosies for the teapots. Soon, we were having tea cosies sent in from all over the country and began featuring them on our website. We have a 'Tea Cosy of the Week' competition, with the winner being sent a few cases of jam. Over time, the cosies have become more and more elaborate and creative – some are in the shape of people, animals or fruits. Knitting has become one of the main activities of the SuperJam tea parties and, a few months after setting up the project, we ran a massive nationwide 'knitathon'. Guests at the hundred or so subsequent tea parties were asked to knit squares. These were then sewn together to make more than a hundred blankets for disabled Indian orphans.

The SuperJam tea parties are a project I am really ambitious about, and even though we now run events nationwide and thousands of elderly people come along, I want it to become bigger and better over the coming years.

I'm spurred on by the feedback that the elderly guests give me. Sometimes the guests have had so much fun that they cry at the end of the afternoon. Most touchingly, one elderly gentleman told me that he 'felt like a person again' after coming along to a few of the events. He had been given the opportunity to socialise and make new friends, something he hadn't done in a long time.

in this book . . .

I'd like to share with you some of the things I've learned about the art of making jam and other preserves. I'm going to take you on a journey through the levels of difficulty. We'll start out with some easy peasies and then go on to more adventurous flavours, but only once you've mastered the basics …

before we get started

(Let's get a couple of things straight before we start chopping things up)

the tools of the trade

Making jam doesn't have to be very scientific – some folks go a bit over the top with thermometers and pH measuring gadgets when they're making jam, but I think there's only a few things you're going to need:

Some large pots and pans.

A funnel – this is for pouring the jam into the jars without it going all over the place. It's also handy if you want to go to a fancy dress party as the Tin Man from *The Wizard of Oz*.

Some old jars – drink lots of coffee, eat plenty of pickle and put mayonnaise on everything, as you'll need to collect some empty jars. In the recipes I have based the jar sizes on standard 454g (1lb) jars – of course, if you use smaller jars expect the recipes to fill more of them; fewer if your jars are bigger.

Pectin – this occurs naturally in a lot of fruit and is what makes jam set. It's like gelatine, but from fruit. Most fruits that have seeds (like raspberries), stones (plums), cores (apples) or tough skins (oranges) contain plenty of pectin. Sometimes you'll need to add more to make sure the jam isn't too runny. You can buy pectin in a bottle at the supermarket (the

brand name is Certo), in the section where the home baking stuff is. I suggest using it in all the recipes but you won't always need to. The best thing to do is follow the recipe and, at the end, check to see if the jam sets (I will explain how later). If it does, you're good to go. If not, you can add a 150ml bottle of pectin, boil up the mixture again for about a minute and the mixture will be almost guaranteed to set.

A jelly bag – as the name suggests, you're only going to need to get one of these when you want to make jelly. It looks like a witch's hat and you hang it over a pot to strain juices from fruit.

some important notes about sterilising and storage

Before you fill all these odd-shaped pots you've collected with your homemade jam, you will need to clean them thoroughly so that it's safe to put the jam into them.

here's the best way to do this:

You should rinse your jars and pop them into an oven set to 200°C/gas mark 6 for 15 minutes, until they are too hot to touch with your hand. You can have them heating up in the oven while you're making the jam, so that they will be completely sterile. If they aren't spotlessly clean, your jam might go mouldy. Also, if they are not hot when you pour the jam into them, there is a risk that they might crack because of the heat.

Make sure you also sterilise your jar lids by putting them into a pan of boiling water for a few minutes, to be sure they are completely clean too. Fill the jars with jam and put the lids on while everything is still hot.

Usually, if you have sterilised everything properly, jams, marmalades and jellies will keep for up to a year before you open them (2 months in the fridge once you have), and curds will last a few weeks in the fridge (these contain butter and egg, so it's best not to have them hanging around for much longer). With the chutneys and special spreads, like nut butters, later on in the book, I've given more detailed storage instructions at the end of each recipe.

your first pot of jam

(An easy peasy one to get you off the ground)

I want to start you off with a simple recipe that
won't take you very long to make and will help you
get a feel for how to make jam if you've never done
it before. Although this isn't a SuperJam (see page 9),
as it uses sugar rather than fruit juice, it's a good
'practice' recipe. This jam tastes great on toast,
in scones or maybe in the middle of a homemade
Victoria sponge (the recipe for that comes on
page 150).

It's best to use a mixture of ripe and slightly under-
ripe fruit. This helps make the jam set, as under-ripe
fruit contains more pectin (see page 16). You can use
frozen or fresh fruit. Over-ripe fruit doesn't work
too well.

summer fruit jam

This is a really great recipe because you can use up whatever berries you have available. Feel free to use more or less of each of the types of fruit or even miss some out entirely. You could add blackberries or blueberries or anything else you have handy.

MAKES ABOUT 6–8 JARS

300g raspberries
300g strawberries
300g blackcurrants
100g redcurrants
1 tablespoon lemon juice
1kg sugar (you can use 'jam-making sugar', which has pectin added to it already, or granulated)
a 150ml bottle of pectin

Step 1: Rinse and chop up the fruit and pop it all into a large pan, along with the lemon juice. Put it on a low heat for about 20–30 minutes, stirring occasionally so it doesn't burn. You just want to make the fruit very tender and reduce it all to a smooth paste, so that it looks kind of like porridge.

Step 2: Meanwhile, spread the sugar out on a baking tray and place it in a warm oven for about 10 minutes. You don't want to cook the sugar, just warm it up. (This is so that it will dissolve quickly into the fruit when you add it.) You want to cook the fruit for as little time as possible, otherwise you will destroy its flavour and nutrients.

Step 3: Add the warm sugar to the fruit mixture and continue to cook on a low heat until the sugar has dissolved. Now you can turn up the heat and raise the mixture to a 'rolling boil', sometimes called the 'setting point' (about 105°C). The jam will be bubbling a lot. Cook it at that level for about a minute.

Step 4: Turn down the heat and let the jam cool for about 5 minutes. Add the pectin and bring back to the boil for another minute.

Step 5: Once you think it has reached 105°C – the jam will be bubbling vigorously (you can use a thermometer if you like) – turn off the heat and test to see if it is going to set. The best method for doing this is to put a spoonful of the jam on a cold plate. It will cool down quickly and if you give it a push with your finger and it wrinkles, that means the jam will set. If it doesn't wrinkle, bring it back to a rolling boil for about a minute and repeat the test.

Step 6: If froth has built up on top of the jam, which sometimes happens and isn't anything to worry about, skim it off. You can also add a knob of butter and give it a stir, which will get rid of the froth.

Step 7: Pour the jam into hot, sterilised jars straight away. Place the lids on the jars before the jam has cooled. This will mean that the jam is completely sterile and will keep for about a year before you open it.

what is a SuperJam?

(Why using fruit juice instead of sugar is a smart idea)

When my gran originally made jam, she had quite
a few tricks and secrets, many of which I am sharing
with you in this book. Wonderful as her jam was,
it was always made with added sugar, which is, of
course, the way that jam is conventionally sweetened.
Sales of jam have been in decline the world over for
the past couple of decades. A lot of this decline can
be blamed on the fact that jam tends to be a very
unhealthy and generally sickly-sweet product. Jam
is usually made with 60–70 per cent sugar and often
with additives, such as preservatives and sweeteners.
Luckily, at quite an early stage in my jam-based
adventures, I decided to change all that. As my
business grew and I was making up to a thousand
jars of homemade jam from my parents' tiny kitchen,
it became necessary for me to think about how I was
going to grow beyond the confines of those walls.
I soon decided that I wanted to reinvent my gran's
recipes, by replacing the sugar with a more natural
sweetener.

I spent hundreds of hours playing around in the
kitchen, trying out dozens of different ideas and
countless recipes. I tried using honey as a sweetener,
then dried fruit and all manner of other things, until
I settled upon grape juice. I realised that juice is ideal

because it helps to emphasise the fruity flavour of the jam, is not too expensive and, as a major bonus, allows you to make a jam that is much lower in sugar than regular jams.

In the recipes throughout the rest of this book, I will explain how to use fruit juice as a natural sweetener for jams. I'll also tell you how much sugar you should use, if you would prefer to make your jam in the usual way.

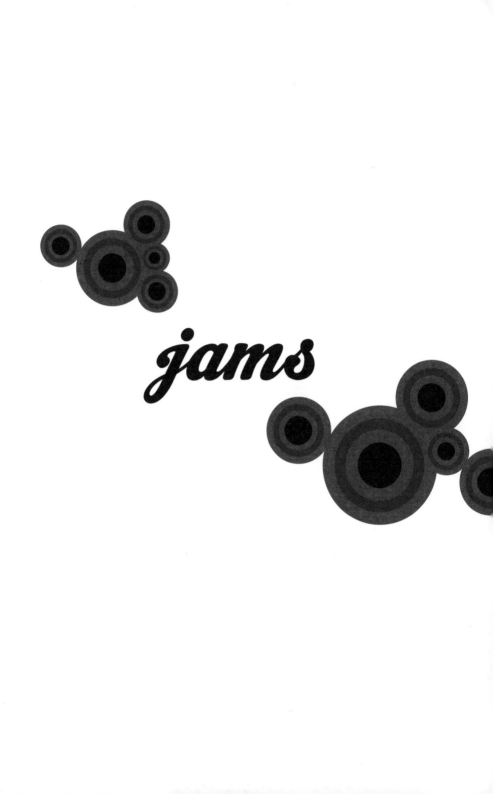

jams

Jam is what this book is about; it's what my whole life is about. You can make it from almost any kind of fruit, savoury or sweet, with added sugar or without. First of all I'd like to share with you the recipes for the SuperJams that we sell in the supermarkets, which maybe you have already had the pleasure of tasting! Hopefully you can give them a shot and then perhaps try out making jam from more adventurous fruits, using the recipes in this book or maybe even your own ideas.

blueberry and blackcurrant SuperJam

This is our bestselling flavour of SuperJam and, if you've tried it, you'll probably be thinking 'and so it should be', since it does taste marvellous. Blueberries are packed with antioxidants and all kinds of good things. In the US, blackcurrants aren't very widely available: growing currants was outlawed in the early 1900s because it was seen as a threat to the logging industry – blackcurrant farmers were buying up land that would otherwise have been used for logging. A few states have since legalised blackcurrants but if you're living somewhere that has banished them, you can replace them with blackberries or just use all blueberries.

MAKES ABOUT 6–8 JARS

3 litres white grape juice
450g blueberries
450g blackcurrants
1 tablespoon lemon juice
a 150ml bottle of pectin

Step 1: Pour the white grape juice into a pan and cook on a medium heat for about 30 minutes, until it has been reduced to about a quarter of its original volume. If you don't do this, your jam will have a weak flavour and probably won't set.

Step 2: While the grape juice is bubbling away, wash the fruit and cut the blueberries in half. Pop the fruit and the lemon juice into another pan and cook gently for about 20 minutes.

Step 3: Once the grape juice has reduced and the fruit is smooth, add the grape juice to the fruit and bring gradually to the boil. Once the jam is boiling, keep it like that for about 5 minutes, watching carefully to prevent it boiling over. At this point, you can test to see if the setting point has been reached by putting a spoonful of jam on a cold plate (see page 23). If it doesn't set, continue to step 4, otherwise you're ready to pour it into hot, sterilised jars!

Step 4: If the jam hasn't set yet, turn down the heat, add the pectin, then bring back to the boil and cook at that heat for a further couple of minutes. Test for the setting point again, and when it's reached you can pour the jam into your jars.

raspberry and cranberry SuperJam

Cranberries are one of those 'superfruits', since they are very high in all kinds of vitamins and minerals, especially antioxidants. My best cranberry fact is about how they are harvested: instead of picking the cranberries off the bushes, the farmers just flood the fields. The cranberries pick themselves off the branches and float to the surface of the water, where the farmers just scoop them up. How clever!

MAKES ABOUT 6–8 JARS

3 litres white grape juice
  (you can use apple juice if you prefer)
700g raspberries
250g cranberries
1 tablespoon lemon juice
a 150ml bottle of pectin

Step 1: Pour the white grape juice into a pan and cook on a medium heat for about 30 minutes. The aim is to reduce the liquid to about a quarter of its original volume (about 750ml).

Step 2: While the grape juice is bubbling away, wash the fruit and chop the cranberries. Pop the fruit and the lemon juice into another pan and cook gently for about 20 minutes.

Step 3: Once the grape juice has reduced and the fruit is smooth, add the grape juice to the fruit and bring gradually to the boil. Once the jam is boiling, keep it like that for about 5 minutes, watching carefully to prevent it boiling over. At this point, you can test to see if the setting point has been reached by putting a spoonful of jam on a cold plate (see page 23). If it doesn't set, continue to step 4, otherwise you're ready to pour it into hot, sterilised jars!

Step 4: If the jam hasn't set yet, turn down the heat, add the pectin, then bring back to the boil and cook at that heat for a further couple of minutes. Test for the setting point again, and when it's reached you can pour the jam into your jars.

jams

strawberry and pomegranate SuperJam

Originally, I didn't want to make a plain old strawberry jam, since SuperJam is all about reinventing jam and doing things differently from everyone else, but apparently more than half of all the jam sold is strawberry. Having realised that we would have to make a strawberry jam, I experimented with adding all sorts of other fruits to make it taste a bit more exciting. Pomegranates have a flavour that complements strawberries well and, as an added benefit, they are packed with lots of goodness.

MAKES ABOUT 6-8 JARS

3 litres white grape juice
900g strawberries
100ml pure pomegranate juice
1 tablespoon lemon juice
a 150ml bottle of pectin

Step 1: Pour the white grape juice into a pan and cook on a medium heat for about 30 minutes, until it has been reduced to about a quarter of its original volume.

Step 2: While the grape juice is gently bubbling away, wash the strawberries and cut them in half. It is best to use small ones, which have a lot more flavour – the big juicy ones just break up in the pan and don't taste of much. Pop the strawberries, along with the pomegranate and lemon juice, into another pan and cook gently for about 20 minutes.

Step 3: Once the grape juice has reduced and the fruit is smooth, add the grape juice to the fruit and bring gradually to the boil. Once the jam is boiling, keep it like that for about 5 minutes, watching carefully to prevent it boiling over. At this point, you can test to see if the setting point has been reached by putting a spoonful of jam on a cold plate (see page 23). If it doesn't set, continue to step 4, otherwise you're ready to pour it into hot, sterilised jars!

Step 4: If the jam hasn't set yet, turn down the heat, add the pectin, then bring back to the boil and cook at that heat for a further couple of minutes. Test for the setting point again, and when it's reached you can pour the jam into your jars.

rhubarb and ginger

This is one of those jams that remind people of their grandmothers, since it is quite an old-fashioned flavour, but it's still a favourite. A lot of people don't like ginger, and if you're one of them, you could just leave it out or perhaps try adding some strawberries instead, which also makes quite a nice jam.

MAKES ABOUT 6-8 JARS

3 litres white grape juice or 1kg sugar
800g rhubarb
100g root ginger, grated
a 150ml bottle of pectin
1 tablespoon lemon juice

Step 1: If you're using grape juice, pour it into a pan and cook on a medium heat for about 30 minutes, until it has been reduced to about a quarter of its original volume.

Step 2: Wash the rhubarb, chop it into small chunks and put it into a pan with the grape juice.

Step 3: If you're using sugar, put some rhubarb into a pan, then a layer of sugar, then some more rhubarb. Let it sit for a couple of hours to allow the rhubarb juices to soak into the sugar.

Step 4: Add the ginger to the pan and cook the rhubarb on a low heat until it has softened quite a lot, for around half an hour. Then raise the heat and, once the jam is boiling, keep it like that for about 5 minutes, watching carefully to prevent it boiling over. At this point, you can test to see if the setting point has been reached by putting a spoonful of jam on a cold plate (see page 23). If it doesn't set, continue to step 4, otherwise you're ready to pour it into hot, sterilised jars!

Step 4: If the jam hasn't set yet, turn down the heat, add the pectin, then bring back to the boil and cook for a further couple of minutes. Test for the setting point again, and when it's reached you can pour the jam into your jars.

pear and guava

Pears are great because they're cheap as chips and are, in my opinion, the apple's better-tasting cousin. This particular jam is nice with soft cheeses or pork. If you can't get hold of guavas, try using papaya or melon.

MAKES ABOUT 6–8 JARS

3 litres white grape juice or 1kg sugar
500g pears
400g guavas
1 tablespoon lemon juice
a 150ml bottle of pectin

Step 1: If you're using grape juice, pour it into a pan and cook on a medium heat for about 30 minutes, until it has been reduced to about a quarter of its original volume. Alternatively, heat the sugar (see page 22).

Step 2: Peel the pears and guavas and chop into small cubes. Put them into a pan with the lemon juice and cook on a medium heat for around 20 minutes, until the fruit has reduced to the consistency of porridge.

Step 3: Add the grape juice or the sugar to the fruit and bring gradually to the boil. Once the jam is boiling, keep it like that for about 5 minutes, watching carefully to prevent it boiling over. At this point, you can test to see if the setting point has been reached by putting a spoonful of jam on a cold plate (see page 23). If it doesn't set, continue to step 4, otherwise you're ready to pour it into hot, sterilised jars!

Step 4: If the jam hasn't set yet, turn down the heat, add the pectin, then bring back to the boil and cook at that heat for a further couple of minutes. Test for the setting point again, and when it's reached you can pour the jam into your jars.

peach and vanilla

As you will no doubt have noticed, vanilla, especially in the form of vanilla pods, is very expensive. It is actually the second most expensive spice in the world, after saffron. Vanilla comes from an orchid originally found in Mexico, where a native bee pollinates it. To grow vanilla on a large scale around the world, the flowers have to be pollinated by hand by a person – which is what makes it so expensive. It tastes great as an ingredient in all kinds of jams: strawberry, pear and especially peach.

MAKES ABOUT 6–8 JARS

1kg sugar or 3 litres white grape juice
900g peaches
2 or 3 vanilla pods
1 tablespoon lemon juice
a 150ml bottle of pectin

Step 1: If you're using grape juice, pour it into a pan and cook on a medium heat for about 30 minutes, until it has been reduced to about a quarter of its original volume. Alternatively, heat the sugar (see page 22).

Step 2: Put the peaches into boiling water for about 30 seconds, then pick them out. It will be easy to remove the skins once you've done that. Chop the peaches into small cubes, keeping the stones to one side (we're going to use them in the recipe because they contain a lot of pectin, which will help your jam set). Put the peaches into a pan, along with their stones and the vanilla pods and lemon juice, and cook on a medium heat for around 20 minutes, until the fruit has reduced to the consistency of porridge.

Step 3: Add the grape juice or sugar to the fruit and bring gradually to the boil. Once the jam is boiling, keep it like that for about 5 minutes, watching carefully to prevent it boiling over. At this point, you can test to see if the setting point has been reached by putting a spoonful of jam on a cold plate (see page 23). If it doesn't set, continue to step 4, otherwise you're ready to pour it into hot, sterilised jars!

Step 4: If the jam hasn't set yet, turn down the heat, add the pectin, then bring back to the boil and cook at that heat for a further couple of minutes. Test for the setting point again, and when it's reached you can pour the jam into your jars.

melon *and lemon*

During the war, most fruits weren't widely available because of shortages and rationing. However, melon and lemon jam was on sale (packaged in tins rather than jars), and we get dozens of people requesting that we start making it, since it reminds them of their wartime childhood. We've not rushed this one into production but I thought it would be nice to include a recipe for it in this book. It actually tastes very refreshing and is nice dolloped onto a bowl of yoghurt.

MAKES ABOUT 6–8 JARS

3 litres white grape juice or 1kg sugar
800g white melon (about 2 melons)
3–4 lemons
a 150ml bottle of pectin

Step 1: If you're using grape juice, pour it into a pan and cook on a medium heat for about 30 minutes, until it has been reduced to about a quarter of its original volume. Allow the juice to cool.

Step 2: Peel and deseed the melon, chop into small cubes and put into a bowl, along with the grape juice or sugar. Leave for a few hours, preferably overnight.

Step 3: Zest and juice the lemons and put into a pan with the melon mixture. Cook on a low heat for around 30 minutes, until it is quite thick, then raise the heat to medium and bring to the boil. Once the jam is boiling, keep it like that for about 5 minutes, watching carefully to prevent it boiling over. At this point, you can test to see if the setting point has been reached by putting a spoonful of jam on a cold plate (see page 23). If it doesn't set, continue to step 4, otherwise you're ready to pour it into hot, sterilised jars!

Step 4: If the jam hasn't set yet, turn down the heat, add the pectin, then bring back to the boil and cook at that heat for a further couple of minutes. Test for the setting point again, and when it's reached you can pour the jam into your jars.

jams

kiwi fruit, lime and ginger

I came up with this recipe when I was about sixteen. The local football team, Hibernian FC, wanted to sell something funny in their gift shop. Their colour is green, while that of their local rivals, Hearts, is red. Hearts' nickname is 'the jam tarts', so making a green jam for Hibernian was a play on that. I started supplying the gift shop with kiwi, lime and ginger jam, which has a really vibrant green colour. It flew off the shelves and the local papers loved the joke.

MAKES ABOUT 6–8 JARS

3 litres white grape juice or 1kg sugar
800g kiwi fruits (about 20 kiwis)
6 limes
50g root ginger, grated
a 150ml bottle of pectin

Step 1: If you're using grape juice, pour it into a pan and cook on a medium heat for about 30 minutes, until it has been reduced to about a quarter of its original volume. Alternatively, heat the sugar (see page 22).
Step 2: Peel and chop the kiwi fruits, and zest and juice the limes. Put all this into a pan, along with the grated ginger. Cook gently on a low heat for about 20 minutes.
Step 3: Once the the fruit is smooth, add the grape juice or sugar to the fruit and bring gradually to the boil. Once the jam is boiling, keep it like that for about 5 minutes, watching carefully to prevent it boiling over. At this point, you can test to see if the setting point has been reached by putting a spoonful of jam on a cold plate (see page 23). If it doesn't set, continue to step 4, otherwise you're ready to pour it into hot, sterilised jars!
Step 4: If the jam hasn't set yet, turn down the heat, add the pectin, then bring back to the boil and cook at that heat for a further couple of minutes. Test for the setting point again, and when it's reached you can pour the jam into your jars.

jams

plum and elderberry

In ancient folklore, the elder tree (which is where elderflowers and elderberries come from) was believed to ward off evil spirits. If the tree was cut down, the 'Elder Mother' spirit would get very angry and unleash her powers on the people who cut it down. The berries from the tree are very good in jam and the flowers can be used in some recipes too. Elderflowers are popular for making cordials.

MAKES ABOUT 6–8 JARS

3 litres white grape juice or 1kg sugar
900g plums
100g elderberries
1 tablespoon lemon juice
a 150ml bottle of pectin

Step 1: If you're using grape juice, pour it into a pan and cook on a medium heat for about 30 minutes, until it has been reduced to about a quarter of its original volume. Alternatively, heat the sugar (see page 22).

Step 2: Chop the plums, keeping their stones to one side. Put the fruit into a pan, along with the stones from the plums, the elderberries and the lemon juice. The stones in the plums contain a lot of pectin and will help your jam to set. Cook on a low heat for about 20 minutes.

Step 3: Once the fruit is smooth, add the grape juice or sugar and bring gradually to the boil. Once the jam is boiling, keep it like that for 5 minutes, watching carefully to prevent it boiling over. At this point, you can test to see if the setting point has been reached by putting a spoonful of jam on a cold plate (see page 23). If it doesn't set, continue to step 4, otherwise you're ready to pour it into hot, sterilised jars!

Step 4: If the jam hasn't set yet, turn down the heat, add the pectin, then bring back to the boil and cook at that heat for a further couple of minutes. Test for the setting point again, and when it's reached you can pour the jam into your jars.

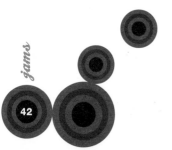

jams

fig

Although it looks like a fruit, a fig is actually a flower. The flower blooms inside the fig and gets pollinated by a special wasp called, surprisingly, a fig wasp. She wriggles her way into the fig and pollinates it, which means that it can grow seeds and become the 'fruit' that we know. Amazing.

MAKES 6–8 JARS

3 litres white grape juice or 1kg sugar
900g fresh figs (about 20 figs)
1 tablespoon lemon juice
a 150ml bottle of pectin

Step 1: If you're using grape juice, pour it into a pan and cook on a medium heat for about 30 minutes, until it has been reduced to about a quarter of its original volume. Alternatively, heat the sugar (see page 22).

Step 2: Wash the figs, then chop off their tops and bottoms and peel them – or you can leave the skins on if you prefer, depending on how ripe the fruit is. Chop them up and pop them into a pan with the lemon juice. Cook gently on a low heat for around 20 minutes.

Step 3: Once the the fruit is smooth, add the grape juice or sugar to the fruit and bring gradually to the boil. Once the jam is boiling, keep it like that for about 5 minutes, watching carefully to prevent it boiling over. At this point, you can test to see if the setting point has been reached by putting a spoonful of jam on a cold plate (see page 23). If it doesn't set, continue to step 4, otherwise you're ready to pour it into hot, sterilised jars!

Step 4: If the jam hasn't set yet, turn down the heat, add the pectin, then bring back to the boil and cook at that heat for a further couple of minutes. Test for the setting point again, and when it's reached you can pour the jam into your jars.

jams

mango *and apple*

In this country, we don't often come across jams that are made from tropical fruits – most are made from berries. In Africa, South America and elsewhere in the world, using tropical fruits like pineapples and mangoes is common – and they make great jam, so I definitely think you should give them a shot.

MAKES ABOUT 6-8 JARS

3 litres white grape juice or 1kg sugar
500g mangoes (about 4 large mangoes)
500g cooking apples (about 3 apples)
1 teaspoon lemon juice
a 150ml bottle of pectin

Step 1: If you're using grape juice, pour it into a pan and cook on a medium heat for about 30 minutes, until it has been reduced to about a quarter of its original volume. Alternatively, heat the sugar (see page 22).
Step 2: Peel the mangoes and apples and chop them into small cubes. Put them into a pan with the lemon juice and cook gently on a low heat for about 20 minutes.
Step 3: Once the the fruit is smooth, add the grape juice or sugar to the fruit and bring gradually to the boil. Once the jam is boiling, keep it like that for about 5 minutes, watching carefully to prevent it boiling over. At this point, you can test to see if the setting point has been reached by putting a spoonful of jam on a cold plate (see page 23). If it doesn't set, continue to step 4, otherwise you're ready to pour it into hot, sterilised jars!
Step 4: If the jam hasn't set yet, turn down the heat, add the pectin, then bring back to the boil and cook at that heat for a further couple of minutes. Test for the setting point again, and when it's reached you can pour the jam into your jars.

cherries
and berries

This is a very rich and fruity jam, ideal in the middle of a Victoria sponge or in a steamed jam pudding (see pages 150 and 112).

MAKES ABOUT 6–8 JARS

3 litres white grape juice or 1kg sugar
500g cherries
200g raspberries
200g blackberries
1 tablespoon lemon juice
a 150ml bottle of pectin

Step 1: If you're using grape juice, pour it into a pan and cook on a medium heat for about 30 minutes, until it has been reduced to about a quarter of its original volume. Alternatively, heat the sugar (see page 22).
Step 2: Remove the stalks and stones from the cherries and discard. Chop up the cherries, and put into a pan along with the raspberries, blackberries and lemon juice. Cook gently on a low heat for around 20 minutes.
Step 3: Once the fruit is smooth, add the grape juice or sugar and bring gradually to the boil. Once the jam is boiling, keep it like that for 5 minutes, watching carefully to prevent it boiling over. At this point, you can test to see if the setting point has been reached by putting a spoonful of jam on a cold plate (see page 23). If it doesn't set, continue to step 4, otherwise you're ready to pour it into hot, sterilised jars!
Step 4: If the jam hasn't set yet, turn down the heat, add the pectin, then bring back to the boil and cook at that heat for a further couple of minutes. Test for the setting point again, and when it's reached you can pour the jam into your jars.

apricot, almond and cinnamon

Every year, more than a million beehives (half of all the beehives in the USA) are trucked across the country to California, to pollinate the almond groves. Most of the world's almond trees are there, and moving all these bees around is the biggest managed pollination anywhere in the world. It is quite an amazing thing. I'm a huge fan of almonds, and using them in jam probably seems strange but it definitely tastes great. The cinnamon makes this a very festive-tasting jam.

MAKES ABOUT 6-8 JARS

3 litres white grape juice or 1kg sugar
900g apricots
1 tablespoon lemon juice
2 teaspoons almond extract
½ teaspoon ground cinnamon
a 150ml bottle of pectin

Step 1: If you're using grape juice, pour it into a pan and cook on a medium heat for about 30 minutes, until it has been reduced to about a quarter of its original volume. Alternatively, heat the sugar (see page 22).

Step 2: Stone and chop the apricots, setting the stones aside. Put the fruit into a pan along with the apricot stones and lemon juice and cook gently on a low heat for around 20 minutes. Stir in the almond extract and cinnamon.

Step 3: Once the fruit is smooth, add the grape juice or sugar to the fruit and bring gradually to the boil. Once the jam is boiling, keep it like that for 5 minutes, watching carefully to prevent it boiling over. At this point, you can test to see if the setting point has been reached (see page 23). If it doesn't set, continue to step 4, otherwise you're ready to pour it into hot, sterilised jars!

Step 4: If the jam hasn't set yet, turn down the heat, add the pectin, then bring back to the boil and cook at that heat for a further couple of minutes. Test for the setting point again, and when it's reached you can pour the jam into your jars.

jams

pineapple

Pineapples are a great fruit, and not just for pizzas and gammon steaks; they make a tasty jam that you can use in your homemade jam tarts (see page 125) or as a glaze for a joint, if you're feeling adventurous.

MAKES ABOUT 6–8 JARS

3 litres white grape juice or 1kg sugar
800g fresh pineapple, skin and core removed
1 tablespoon lemon juice
a 150ml bottle of pectin

Step 1: If you're using grape juice, pour it into a pan and cook on a medium heat for about 30 minutes, until it has been reduced to about a quarter of its original volume. Alternatively, heat the sugar (see page 22).

Step 2: Chop the pineapple, removing any tough parts, and put into a pan with the lemon juice. Cook gently on a low heat for around 20 minutes.

Step 3: Once the fruit is smooth, add the grape juice or sugar to the fruit and bring gradually to the boil. Once the jam is boiling, keep it like that for about 5 minutes, watching carefully to prevent it boiling over. At this point, you can test to see if the setting point has been reached by putting a spoonful of jam on a cold plate (see page 23). If it doesn't set, continue to step 4, otherwise you're ready to pour it into hot, sterilised jars!

Step 4: If the jam hasn't set yet, turn down the heat, add the pectin, then bring back to the boil and cook at that heat for a further couple of minutes. Test for the setting point again, and when it's reached you can pour the jam into your jars.

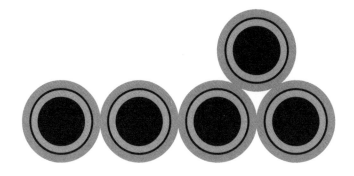

marmalades

Marmalades are like jams but are generally quite bitter, since they are made from citrus fruits. They're mostly eaten at breakfast. Marmalade, in the form we know it, was invented by the Keiller family of Dundee, Scotland. In the late 1700s they began selling homemade 'Dundee Marmalade' from their sweet shop in the city. It was a phenomenal success and they soon built a factory to meet demand. Jam and marmalade were eventually one of the major industries of the city, which is often described as 'the home of jute, journalism and jam'.

Over the past couple of hundred years, marmalade in the style that the Keillers invented has become popular the world over, most notably with travelling Peruvian bears.

Your homemade marmalades will keep in sterilised jars in the cupboard for around a year before opening.

ginger

Making a marmalade entirely from ginger gives you one that has a very intense flavour, and you can make it as spicy as you like by adding more or less root ginger. The marmalade ends up looking like a clear grey jelly and is great as a glaze for meats or in the bottom of tarts.

MAKES ABOUT 6–8 JARS

3 litres white grape juice or 1 kg sugar
200g root ginger
500ml water
1 tablespoon lemon juice
a 150ml bottle of pectin

Step 1: If you're using grape juice, pour it into a pan and cook on a medium heat for about 30 minutes, until it has been reduced to about a quarter of its original volume. Alternatively, heat the sugar (see page 22).
Step 2: After you have removed the skin of the root ginger, finely slice or grate it so that you have long strands.
Step 3: Put the ginger into a pan, along with the water and lemon juice, and cook on a low heat for about 20 minutes, until the mixture has reduced and the water tastes very gingery. Add the warm sugar or grape juice and bring to a rolling boil for about a minute. At this point, you can test to see if the setting point has been reached by putting a spoonful of marmalade on a cold plate (see page 23). If it doesn't set, continue to step 4, otherwise you're ready to pour it into hot, sterilised jars!
Step 4: If the marmalade hasn't set yet, turn down the heat, add the pectin, then bring back to the boil and cook at that heat for a further couple of minutes. Test for the setting point again, and when it's reached you can pour the jam into your jars.

Seville orange and Scotch

Seville oranges are the classic marmalade fruit. They are quite big oranges and contain a lot of pectin, which makes them ideal for the purpose. Seville oranges aren't available fresh all the year round, and we can only buy them from December to February. Processed, tinned Seville oranges can be bought from the supermarket at any time of year, but this isn't nearly as good as using fresh oranges. So you'll need to schedule your marmalade-making to catch the Sevilles when they're around.

MAKES ABOUT 6–8 JARS

3 litres white grape juice or 1kg sugar
4 Seville oranges
750ml water
a 150ml bottle of pectin
2 tablespoons Scotch whisky

Step 1: If you're using grape juice, pour it into a pan and cook on a medium heat for about 30 minutes, until it has been reduced to about a quarter of its original volume. Alternatively, heat the sugar (see page 22).

Step 2: Cut the oranges in half, scoop out the flesh and blend in a food processor. Scoop out as much of the pith from the orange skins as possible, then finely slice the rinds.

Step 3: Press the blended flesh through a sieve into a pan. Add the water and sliced rinds and cook on a low heat until they soften.

Step 4: Add the grape juice or warm sugar and bring to a rolling boil for about a minute. At this point, you can test to see if the setting point has been reached by putting a spoonful of marmalade on a cold plate (see page 23). If it doesn't set, continue to step 5, otherwise let the pan cool a little before adding the whisky and you're ready to pour it into hot, sterilised jars!

Step 5: If the marmalade hasn't set yet, turn down the heat, add the pectin, then bring back to the boil for a further couple of minutes. Test for the setting point again, then follow the rest of step 4.

marmalades

orange and passion fruit

This is the marmalade that we sell as part of the SuperJam range, and I think it tastes amazing (I guess I would say that though, wouldn't I?). After trying oranges mixed with all kinds of different fruits and flavours, I decided that passion fruits work best, although combining oranges with other citrus fruit (like kumquats and lemons) is also worth trying out.

MAKES ABOUT 6–8 JARS

3 litres white grape juice or 1kg sugar
2 Seville oranges
2 sweet oranges
2 passion fruits
750ml water
1 tablespoon lemon juice
a 150ml bottle of pectin

Step 1: If you're using grape juice, pour it into a pan and cook on a medium heat for about 30 minutes, until it has been reduced to about a quarter of its original volume. Alternatively, heat the sugar (see page 22).

Step 2: Halve all the oranges and scoop out the flesh into a food processor. Scoop out the insides of the passion fruits, sieve to remove the seeds then add to the food processor and blend. Scoop out as much of the pith from the orange skins as possible, then finely slice the rinds.

Step 3: Press the blended fruit through a sieve into a pan. Add the water and the sliced rinds and cook on a low heat until they soften.

Step 4: Add the grape juice or warm sugar and bring to a rolling boil for about a minute. At this point, you can test to see if the setting point has been reached (see page 23). If it doesn't set, continue to step 5, otherwise you're ready to pour it into hot, sterilised jars!

Step 5: If the marmalade hasn't set, lower the heat, add the pectin, then bring back to the boil and cook for two minutes. Test for the setting point and when it's reached pour into your jars.

marmalades

lemon
and lime

Lemons and limes are one of the longstanding, time-tested partnerships, like fish and chips, bangers and mash, Tom and Jerry and Corona and lime.

MAKES ABOUT 6–8 JARS

3 litres white grape juice or 1kg sugar
4 lemons
4 limes
750ml water
a 150ml bottle of pectin

Step 1: If you're using grape juice, pour it into a pan and cook on a medium heat for about 30 minutes, until it has been reduced to about a quarter of its original volume. Alternatively, heat the sugar (see page 22).

Step 2: Cut the lemons and limes in half, scoop out the flesh and blend in a food processor. Scoop out as much of the pith from their skins as possible, then finely slice the rinds.

Step 3: Press the blended flesh through a sieve into a pan. Add the water and the sliced rinds and cook on a low heat until they soften.

Step 4: Add the warm sugar or grape juice and bring to a rolling boil for about a minute. At this point, you can test to see if the setting point has been reached by putting a spoonful of marmalade on a cold plate (see page 23). If it doesn't set, continue to step 5, otherwise you're ready to pour it into hot, sterilised jars!

Step 5: If the marmalade hasn't set yet, turn down the heat, add the pectin, then bring back to the boil and cook at that heat for a further couple of minutes. Test for the setting point again, and when it's reached you can pour the marmalade into your jars.

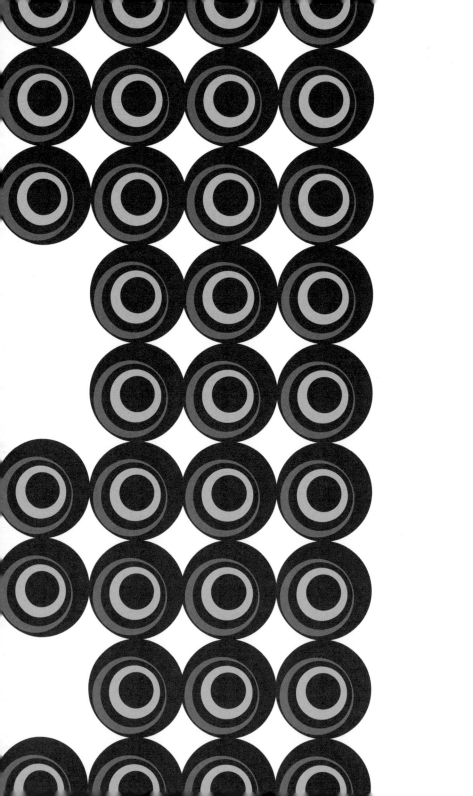

jellies

A jelly is a clear kind of jam that contains no whole fruit and is made by straining the juice out of the cooked fruit using a jelly bag. In years gone by, housewives would use their old stockings as jelly bags but I haven't tried this, since I don't wear stockings very often! You can make jellies (using your old stockings if you really want to) that are sweet or savoury. Savoury jellies, such as redcurrant, often accompany cooked meats, and of course you'll be able to make some lip-smackingly tasty peanut butter and jelly (PBandJ) sandwiches with your sweet jellies.

In all seriousness, if you don't have a jelly bag and can't get your hands on one, you can use a sheet of muslin instead. Your homemade jellies will keep in sterilised jars in the cupboard for about a year.

apple and blackcurrant

This is a great jelly for sweet or savoury dishes. You can have it with your Sunday roast, use it to flavour rice pudding or mousse, or simply have a dollop in yoghurt.

MAKES ABOUT 6–8 JARS

200g blackcurrants
750g apples
3 litres white grape juice or 1kg sugar
a 150ml bottle of pectin
1 tablespoon lemon juice

Step 1: Chop the blackcurrants. Peel the apples and cut into small cubes. Place in a pan on a low heat with a little water and cook gently for 20 minutes, until soft.

Step 2: Pour the fruit mixture into a jelly bag and allow the juices to strain into a large pan. This may take a few hours. You can squeeze the bag to get the last of the juice out, but this may make the jelly cloudy.

Step 3: If you're using grape juice, pour it into a pan and cook on a medium heat for about 30 minutes, until it has been reduced to about a quarter of its original volume. Alternatively, heat the sugar (see page 22).

Step 4: Add the grape juice or sugar to the fruit juices and bring to a rolling boil for about a minute. At this point, you can test to see if the setting point has been reached by putting a spoonful of jelly on a cold plate (see page 23). If it doesn't set, continue to step 5, otherwise you're ready to pour it into hot, sterilised jars!

Step 5: If the jelly hasn't set yet, turn down the heat, add the pectin, then bring back to the boil and cook for a further couple of minutes. Test for the setting point again, and when it's reached you can pour the jelly into your jars.

redcurrant

Redcurrant jelly is another classic, and since it has quite a tart taste, it is great with roast dinners, on turkey sandwiches or as an ingredient in stews.

MAKES ABOUT 6-8 JARS

750g redcurrants
3 litres white grape juice or 1kg sugar
a 150ml bottle of pectin
1 tablespoon lemon juice

Step 1: Since we're making jelly, don't worry about removing the currants from their stalks. Just wash and put them into a pan. Cook gently on a low heat for 15–20 minutes, squashing the currants to release their juices.
Step 2: Pour the fruit into a jelly bag and allow the juices to strain into a large pan. This may take a few hours. You can squeeze the bag to get the last of the juice out but this may make the jelly cloudy.
Step 3: If you're using grape juice, pour it into a pan and cook on a medium heat for about 30 minutes, until it has been reduced to about a quarter of its original volume. Alternatively, heat the sugar (see page 22).
Step 4: Add the grape juice or sugar to the fruit juices and bring to a rolling boil for about a minute. At this point, you can test to see if the setting point has been reached by putting a spoonful of jelly on a cold plate (see page 23). If it doesn't set, continue to step 5, otherwise you're ready to pour it into hot, sterilised jars!
Step 5: If the jelly hasn't set yet, turn down the heat, add the pectin, then bring back to the boil and cook for a further couple of minutes. Test for the setting point again, and when it's reached you can pour the jelly into your jars.

jellies

mint

Mint jelly is, of course, the traditional condiment for lamb. It usually has a bright green colour, because commercial mint jellies have colouring added to them. I don't really like the idea of that, but if you want bright green jelly you can add some colouring to the ingredients.

MAKES ABOUT 6–8 JARS

300g fresh mint leaves
900g tart cooking apples
250ml white vinegar
3 litres white grape juice or 1kg sugar

Step 1: Chop the mint and the apples, including the skins, cores and stalks, in a food processor. Put into a pan and cook gently for 15–20 minutes, making sure that it doesn't burn, until the apple is mushy. Add the vinegar and boil.

Step 2: Pour the fruit mixture into a jelly bag and allow the juices to strain into a large pan. This may take a few hours. You can squeeze the bag to get the last of the juice out but this may make the jelly cloudy.

Step 3: If you're using grape juice, pour it into a pan and cook on a medium heat for about 30 minutes, until it has been reduced to about a quarter of its original volume. Alternatively, heat the sugar (see page 22).

Step 4: Add the grape juice or sugar to the fruit juices and bring to a rolling boil for about a minute. At this point, you can test to see if the setting point has been reached (see page 23). If it doesn't set, continue to step 5, otherwise you're ready to pour it into hot, sterilised jars!

Step 5: If the jelly hasn't set yet, turn down the heat, add the pectin, then bring back to the boil and cook for a further couple of minutes. Test for the setting point again, and when it's reached you can pour the jelly into your jars.

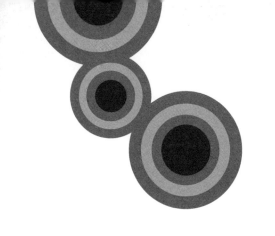

curds

Curds are one of those old-fashioned spreads that you probably don't eat very often but might imagine your gran putting in the middle of her Victoria sponges. They are made from a mixture of eggs, sugar and fruit, and make a great filling for tarts, cakes and pastries or simply for spreading on toast. I'd like to think that some of the recipes here, like the Banana and Rum curd, might make curd a bit more rock 'n' roll.

lemon

Lemon curd is the classic: creamy and tart, with a lovely yellow colour. It makes a great filling for sponges, tarts or even muffins.

MAKES ABOUT 3-4 JARS

3 litres white grape juice or 750g sugar
4 lemons
4 eggs
100g butter

Step 1: If you're using white grape juice, pour it into a pan and cook on a medium heat for about 30 minutes, until it has been reduced to about a quarter of its original volume. Leave to cool.

Step 2: Squeeze the juice from the lemons. You can also use the zest of the lemons, depending on how tart you want your curd to be (adding the zest makes it more tart). You should zest the lemons very finely, so that the curd is nice and smooth.

Step 3: Beat the eggs in a bowl until smooth.

Step 4: Put the eggs, grape juice or sugar, butter, lemon zest and juice into a bowl set on top of a pan of simmering water, over a low heat.

Step 5: Cook the mixture, stirring constantly, until the curd can coat the back of a spoon. Don't raise the temperature too high, otherwise the eggs will cook and make your curd lumpy.

Step 6: Pour the warm mixture into hot, sterilised jars.

strawberry and rose petal

This curd is a bit fancy and has a lovely pink colour. Finding rose petals might be tricky, depending on the time of year – don't be afraid of picking some from your garden (be sure to wash them and check them for any unwanted wriggly stowaways).

MAKES ABOUT 6–8 JARS

3 litres white grape juice or 750g sugar
200g strawberries
50g rose petals
4 eggs
100g butter

Step 1: If you're using white grape juice, pour it into a pan and cook on a medium heat for about 30 minutes, until it has been reduced to about a quarter of its original volume. Leave to cool.

Step 2: Chop the strawberries and rose petals and put into a pan. Cook gently over a low heat until the strawberries have broken down. Pour the mixture through a sieve or jelly bag to extract the juices.

Step 3: Beat the eggs in a bowl until smooth.

Step 4: Put the eggs, grape juice or sugar, butter and fruit juices into a bowl on top of a pan of simmering water, over a low heat.

Step 5: Cook the mixture, stirring constantly, until the curd can coat the back of a spoon.

Step 6: Pour the warm mixture into hot, sterilised jars.

banana
and rum

This is my favourite curd of all time, and it can be used as a filling for homemade cupcakes or just spread on toast. I've written an easy recipe for Banoffee Cupcakes (you'll find it on page 126), which are filled with this curd. Yum!

MAKES ABOUT 6–8 JARS

3 litres white grape juice or 750g sugar
3 bananas
a squeeze of lemon juice
4 eggs
100g butter
1–2 tablespoons rum

Step 1: If you're using white grape juice, pour it into a pan and cook on a medium heat for about 30 minutes, until it has been reduced to about a quarter of its original volume. Leave to cool.

Step 2: Peel and thoroughly mash the bananas. You can use a food processor or a hand blender to make them extra smooth if you like. Add a squeeze of lemon to the banana to help stop it going brown.

Step 3: Beat the eggs in a bowl until smooth.

Step 4: Put the eggs, grape juice or sugar, butter and mashed bananas into a bowl set on top of a pan of simmering water, over a low heat.

Step 5: Cook the mixture, stirring constantly, until the curd can coat the back of a spoon. Turn off the heat and stir in the rum (I like to use Malibu in this recipe).

Step 6: Pour the warm mixture into hot, sterilised jars.

curds

coconut and pineapple

This curd is made very creamy by the coconut milk in the recipe and is inspired by the Piña Colada cocktail. You could, of course, add a splash of rum to the recipe, if you fancy the idea of that.

MAKES ABOUT 6-8 JARS

3 litres white grape juice or 750g sugar
200g pineapple (fresh or tinned)
4 eggs
100g butter
100ml coconut milk

Step 1: If you're using white grape juice, pour it into a pan and cook on a medium heat for about 30 minutes, until it has been reduced to about a quarter of its original volume. Leave to cool.

Step 2: Using a food processor or hand blender, blitz the pineapple until it is a smooth liquid. Pour it through a sieve or jelly bag to extract the juice. (Alternatively, you could buy a carton of pineapple juice, but make sure that it is 100% juice and not made from concentrate.)

Step 3: Beat the eggs in a bowl until smooth.

Step 4: Put the eggs, grape juice or sugar, butter, coconut milk and pineapple juice into a bowl set on top of a pan of simmering water, over a low heat.

Step 5: Cook the mixture, stirring constantly, until the curd can coat the back of a spoon.

Step 6: Pour the warm mixture into hot, sterilised jars.

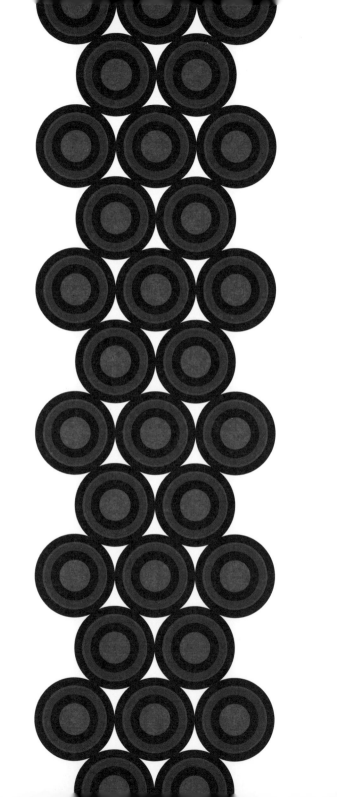

chutneys

Chutneys are basically savoury jams that have spices and vinegars added, so that they taste great with meats, curries, cheeses and in sandwiches. As with jam, there are a million fruits and vegetables out there that you can make them from, but I've chosen to share with you my recipes for some 'classic' chutneys.

Your homemade chutneys will keep in sterilised jars in the cupboard for about a year; they even get better with age and taste best after 6–8 weeks. Once you've opened them, it's best to keep them in the fridge and use them within 2 months.

mango *chutney*

This is the classic chutney served with poppadoms in Indian restaurants the world over. I think it makes a good friend for cold meats in a sandwich or, of course, a curry.

MAKES ABOUT 4-6 JARS

4 mangoes
4 apples
2 onions
4 garlic cloves
600g brown sugar
50g grated root ginger
600ml cider vinegar

Step 1: Getting the flesh off mangoes without making a mess has a knack to it. Probably the easiest way is to cut off the 'cheeks' of the mango at either side of the stone, from the top down. If you score these chunks of mango in a criss-cross pattern, then turn them inside out, you can slice the chunks off the skin very easily.
Step 2: Finely chop the apples, onions and garlic then put everything into a large pan. Let it simmer on a low heat for an hour or so, until the liquid has evaporated, the mango has broken down and you are left with a thick syrupy chutney.
Step 3: Pour the chutney into hot, sterilised jars and let it cool. Ideally, you should leave it for a month or more before you eat it, to mature in flavour.

caramelised *red onion*

This is my favourite chutney. It's wonderful with goat's cheese, on a pizza or in a quiche. It's also at home in a cheese toastie.

MAKES ABOUT 4-6 JARS

8 red onions
1 red chilli
2 bay leaves
25ml olive oil
200g brown sugar
150ml balsamic vinegar
150ml red wine vinegar

Step 1: Cut your onions and chilli into short, thin slices and put them into a pan with the bay leaves and oil. Cook gently over a low heat for about 20 minutes.
Step 2: Once the onions are dark and sticky, add the sugar and the vinegars and simmer for 30 minutes or so, until the chutney is thick and dark.
Step 3: Pour the chutney into hot, sterilised jars and let it cool. Ideally, you should leave it for a month or more before you eat it, to mature in flavour.

apple and date

This is a smashing chutney for accompanying hard cheeses and is quite similar in flavour to the eponymous Branston pickle.

MAKES ABOUT 4–6 JARS

1kg cooking apples
150ml cider vinegar
1 garlic clove
150g dates, stoned
400g brown sugar
50g sultanas
1 clove
a pinch of cayenne pepper

Step 1: Peel and core the apples, then chop them very finely and put them into a pan. Finely chop the garlic and add to the pan with the vinegar. Cook over a low heat until the apples have broken down.
Step 2: Add everything else and cook over a low heat for around 30 minutes, or until the liquid has evaporated and the chutney is thick and dark.
Step 3: Pour the chutney into hot sterilised jars and leave to cool. Ideally, you should leave it for a month or so before you eat it, to mature in flavour.

chutneys

beetroot *and orange*

This chutney has a beautiful, deep purple colour and is delicious with cheeses or meats. You can add spices and mustard to make it a bit more exciting if you want to.

MAKES ABOUT 4–6 JARS

500g onions
1 tbsp olive oil
400g eating apples
4 oranges
1.4kg beetroot
750g brown sugar
750ml cider vinegar

Step 1: Finely chop the onions and put them into a large pan with the oil. Cook gently over a medium heat until soft. Peel and core the apples then chop them very finely and add to the pan along with the zest and juice of the oranges.

Step 2: Once the apples have broken down, finely chop the beetroot then add to the pan along with the sugar and vinegar and cook over a medium heat for about 30 minutes until the chutney is thick and sticky.

Step 3: Pour the chutney into hot, sterilised jars and leave to cool. Ideally, you should leave it for a month or so before you eat it, to mature in flavour.

tomato

This chutney is great with cold meats, in sandwiches or with roasted vegetables.

MAKES ABOUT 4–6 JARS

2 cooking apples
1kg tomatoes
300g onions
1 garlic clove
50g grated root ginger
500ml cider vinegar
250g brown sugar

Step 1: Peel and core the apples, then chop them very finely and put them into a pan. Finely chop the tomatoes, onions and garlic and add to the pan with the ginger. Cook over a low heat until the apples have broken down and most of the liquid has evaporated.
Step 2: Add the vinegar and sugar and cook over a medium heat until the chutney is thick and flavoursome.
Step 3: Pour the chutney into hot, sterilised jars and leave to cool. Ideally, you should leave it for a month or so before you eat it, to mature in flavour.

chutneys

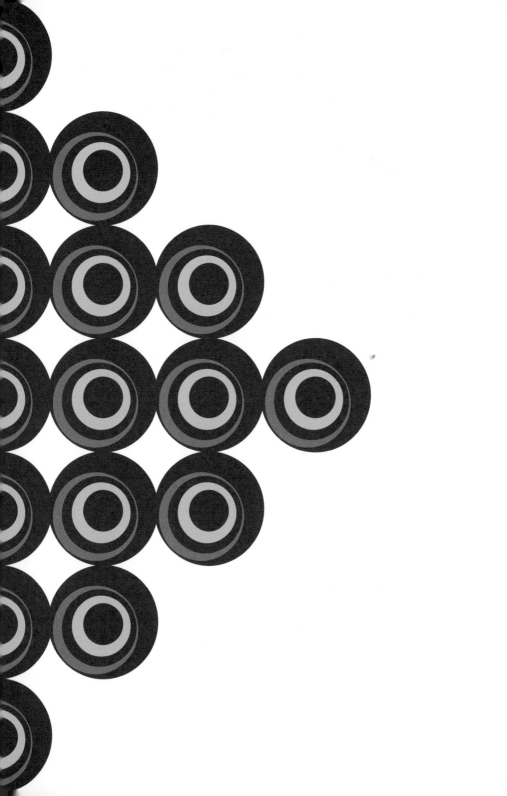

special spreads

One of the things I have found out about jam is that everyone has a story about it. It is something that reminds people about their childhood – there are specific recipes they grew up with that bring back fond memories for them, or new ideas for spreads they have encountered in other countries. Spreads come in lots of different forms, and I wanted to share a few of the more unusual ones that I've come across or invented while I've been playing with ideas.

dulce de leche

Dulce de leche is similar to the French '*confiture de lait*', meaning 'milk jam'. The idea of a jam made of milk is at best quite amusing and at worst probably quite disgusting, but don't be put off. Dulce de leche is actually a rich, thick caramel spread. It is used as a topping for freshly baked bread or croissants, or as a filling for homemade muffins and many other puddings. I personally like it a lot with ice cream. This is quite a basic recipe, but you can add brandy or whisky if you want it to be a bit more flavoursome.

MAKES ABOUT 6–8 JARS

2.5 litres whole milk
650g sugar
1 teaspoon bicarbonate of soda
1 teaspoon salt
1–2 vanilla pods
1–2 tablespoons whisky or brandy (optional)

Step 1: Put the milk, sugar, bicarbonate of soda and salt into a large pan. Scrape the seeds out of the vanilla pods and add to the pan.
Step 2: Bring the mixture to a boil on a medium heat, stirring continuously.
Step 3: Turn the heat down and continue to cook the mixture on a low heat for about 2 hours, stirring and checking on it every once in a while. It might take a bit longer than 2 hours. You are aiming for it to be about a sixth of its original volume, a sort of caramel. Bear in mind that it will thicken up a bit when you put it into the jars.
Step 4: Once you've got it quite thick, add a tablespoon or two of whisky or brandy, if you want to, and give it all a good whisk before putting the mixture into hot, sterilised jars. It will keep for up to 2 months in the fridge, a fortnight once you've opened it, though it will probably be a lot less than that because it's delicious!

chilli jam

I make this recipe quite often, so I thought I'd stick it in the book. It's a very simple savoury jam, as you would imagine, and is great on burgers or grilled chicken. You can make it as hot as you like, depending on the type of chilli you use.

MAKES ABOUT 3-4 JARS

400g cherry tomatoes
9 red peppers
9 red chillies
6 garlic cloves
a thumb-sized chunk of root ginger
700g sugar
200ml cider vinegar

Step 1: Finely chop the tomatoes, peppers, chillies, garlic and ginger. You can use a food processor if you prefer. Don't be daft about touching your eyes or anywhere else that might sting!

Step 2: Put the sugar and vinegar into a pan over a low heat and stir until the sugar is dissolved. Add the tomatoes, peppers, chillies, garlic and ginger and simmer until the liquid has reduced and the mixture has a thick, sticky consistency.

Step 3: Bring to the boil, and cook on high for 1 minute, being careful not to let the jam boil over. Pour the jam into hot, sterilised jars; where it will keep for up to a year, or 1 month in the fridge once you've opened it.

homemade *peanut butter*

Peanut butter is a very simple spread, and making it at home is really straightforward. You can use it alongside your homemade jellies to make some smashing PBandJ sarnies, and I've got a recipe for peanut butter cookies later in the book, which taste great (see page 134).

MAKES ABOUT 6–8 JARS

1kg unsalted peanuts (weight without shells)
150g caster sugar or honey
150ml peanut oil
2 teaspoons salt

Step 1: Put the peanuts, sugar or honey, oil and salt into a food processor and blend until smooth. If you would prefer your peanut butter to be chunky, just blend half the nuts with the sugar, oil and salt until it's smooth. Add the rest of the nuts afterwards and blend by pulsing it, until it is how you like it.

Step 2: Put the peanut butter into warm, sterilised jars and store it in the fridge. It will keep for up to 3 months, or 1 month once you've opened it.

special spreads

black butter

Firstly, black butter (*le nièr beurre*) isn't actually black, it's brown. It also doesn't contain any butter, but you could say that it has the consistency of it. This spread is traditionally made on the island of Jersey, where they also make a lot of cider and probably have a jolly time doing so. In the past, the islanders would have large community events, making black butter in vast quantities for themselves and to sell to visitors. It can be spread on warm bread, eaten on its own or even with ice cream.

MAKES ABOUT 6–8 JARS

2 litres apple cider
1kg sweet apples
1 lemon
150g sugar
1 stick of liquorice
3 teaspoons ground allspice

Step 1: Boil the cider in a pan until it has reduced to about a quarter of its original volume, which should take about 30 minutes on a medium heat.

Step 2: Peel, core and finely chop the apples and add them to the cider. Cook gently for around 1 hour, watching to check that they don't burn, until you have a thick brown butter.

Step 3: Zest and juice the lemon and add to the mixture along with the sugar and liquorice.

Step 4: Cook for about another 10–15 minutes, or until the liquorice dissolves into the mixture. Add the allspice and cook on a low heat for a further 10 minutes.

Step 5: Put the black butter into hot, sterilised jars, where it will keep for up to a year, or 1 month in the fridge once you've opened it.

homemade
chocolate spread

Chocolate spread is always a favourite. There are a lot of different ways to make it, but the recipe I have come up with makes a spread that is quite similar to Nutella. You could use a bar of dark chocolate in place of the cocoa, or perhaps add cream if you wanted it to be smoother. Whichever way you make it, it's great on pancakes, croissants or just on toast. I think the idea of chocolate sandwiches is the epitome of sophistication.

MAKES ABOUT 6–8 JARS

500g hazelnuts
50g butter
250g sugar
100g unsweetened cocoa powder

Step 1: Put the hazelnuts into a food processor and blend thoroughly until smooth.
Step 2: Add the butter and sugar to the processor, along with the cocoa, and blend until it is as silky smooth as you like.
Step 3: Pop it all into warm, sterilised jars and keep them in the fridge, since it has butter in it. Enjoy within 2 weeks. If you want your chocolate spread to keep for longer, you can use two tablespoons of peanut oil in place of the butter.

special spreads

marshmallow crème

Marshmallow crème is popular in the United States, where the main brand, Fluff, is used in puddings and snacks. Kids often make 'fluffernutter' sandwiches, filled with peanut butter and marshmallow crème. You can use it to make snowballs, Rice Krispie bars, fudge or rocky road.

MAKES ABOUT 3-4 JARS

3 egg whites
200g glucose syrup or golden syrup
½ teaspoon salt
200g icing sugar
1 teaspoon vanilla extract

Step 1: Using an electric hand whisk, mix the egg whites, syrup and salt until the mixture thickens.
Step 2: Add the icing sugar and continue to whisk until the mixture starts to look like clouds.
Step 3: Add the vanilla and whisk it in well. The mixture should look like thick shaving foam by now, which is what you're aiming for.
Step 4: Put it into warm, sterilised jars and store in the fridge. It will keep for 3 days, but is best used immediately.

mincemeat

Historically, mincemeat contained minced meat, as you might expect by its name. Of course, it doesn't now (having said that, most mincemeats do contain suet, which is beef fat, although vegetarian suet is widely available as an alternative). You can use this recipe to make delicious mince pies at Christmas and you can add other dried fruits or spirits to the recipe.

MAKES ABOUT 6–8 JARS

350g cooking apples
350g candied peel
350g raisins
350g currants
100g flaked almonds
400g beef suet or vegetarian suet
400g brown sugar
1 teaspoon ground cinnamon
1 teaspoon grated nutmeg
1 teaspoon ground mixed spice
rind and juice of 1 lemon
400ml rum, sherry or brandy

Step 1: Finely chop the apples then put everything into a big ovenproof dish, such as a casserole dish, adding only half the booze. You can use rum, sherry or brandy or a mixture of all of them. Give it all a good mix and leave it to sit for a while, ideally a day, so that the flavours can develop.
Step 2: Put the dish into the oven on a low heat for about 3 hours, until you have thick, sticky, dark mincemeat. You can use it right away, but it tends to taste better if you leave it for a month or more for the flavours to mature.
Step 3: Put it into hot, sterilised jars and it will keep for a year in the cupboard, 1 month once in the fridge once you've opened it.

special spreads

quince *cheese*

Like a sort of solid, thick jelly that you can cut into slices, fruit cheeses like this one are generally served with cheese. You can make them from all kinds of fruit using the same process, but quince is the classic.

MAKES ABOUT 3-4 JARS

1kg quinces
1 lemon
275ml water
600g white sugar

Step 1: Wash and chop the quinces, including their skins and cores. Pop them into a pan along with the juice of the lemon and the water.

Step 2: Bring the mixture to the boil, then put a lid on the pan, reduce the heat and leave it to simmer for about 3 hours, or until the quinces are a dark pink colour. You might need to add more water to stop them burning, so keep checking on it every 20 minutes or so.

Step 3: Once you have a very soft pulp, press it through a fine sieve or a jelly bag to extract the juice. Put the juice into a pan with the sugar and bring to the boil. Cook the mixture until it is thick enough to be able to draw a spoon across the bottom of the pan and still see the bottom afterwards.

Step 4: Store the quince cheese in very clean plastic tubs that you can easily turn it out from when you want to eat it. You might like to use plastic moulds, or interesting shapes, so that when you turn your quince cheese out it will look pretty. It will keep for up to 3 months, or 1 month in the fridge once you've opened it.

homemade *pistachio butter*

You can make butter from any kind of nuts you like, or even from a selection of your favourites. My favourite nuts are pistachios, so I decided to try making a pistachio butter, which turned out a lovely green colour. I think it tastes very nice as a filling between homemade cookies. I've since discovered that pistachio butter is actually quite common in Italy.

MAKES ABOUT 6–8 JARS

1kg unsalted pistachios (weight without shells)
150g caster sugar or honey
350ml peanut oil
2 teaspoons salt

Step 1: Put the pistachios, sugar or honey, oil and salt into a food processor and blend until smooth. If you would prefer your pistachio butter to be chunky, just blend half the nuts with the sugar, oil and salt until it's smooth. Add the rest of the nuts afterwards and blend a little bit, until it is how you like it.
Step 2: Put the butter into warm, sterilised jars and store it in the fridge. It will keep for up to 3 months, or 1 month once you've opened it (or a week if you like it as much as I do!).

jammy treats

Once you get cracking with your homemade jam, you'll no doubt end up making more than you can eat on your morning toast alone. Jam is very versatile, and there are all kinds of puddings that require the use of jams, marmalades and curds, especially classic British puddings like Roly Poly, Arctic Roll and Bakewell Tart.

In the last part of this book, I'm going to share with you my recipes for the classics and also some more adventurous recipes like Macarons and Strawberry and White Chocolate Mousse. You'll soon be having afternoon tea, picnics and dinner parties to share your puddings, cakes and desserts with your friends.

Jam Roly Poly
Jammy Bread and Butter
  Pudding
Queen of Puddings
Raspberry and
  Cranberry Cranachan
Bakewell Tarts
Steamed Jam Pudding
Arctic Roll
Orange and Passion
  Fruit Trifle
Cheesecake
New York Cheesecake
Strawberry and White
  Chocolate Mousse
Raspberry Ripple Ice
  Cream
Jam Tarts
Banoffee Cupcakes

Viennese Swirls
Macarons
Jammy Dodgers
Peanut Butter Cookies
Muffins
Financiers
Jam Doughnuts
Scones (All butter, Apple
  and cinnamon, Treacle)
Blueberry and
  Blackcurrant Oat Slices
Millefeuille
Linzer Bars
Almond Meringue Bars
Victoria Sponge
Battenberg Cake
Rice Pudding
Swiss Roll

jam roly poly
the classic jam pudding

Jam Roly Poly has to be the first recipe in this section of the book. It is, after all, the classic jam pudding. Invented in the early nineteenth century, the dish was also known as 'dead man's arm', since it was often steamed and served in a shirtsleeve. Traditionally, the Roly Poly was served immediately, still bubbling hot, with a generous serving of custard.

SERVES 4–6

200g self-raising flour
100g suet
a pinch of salt
250g jam of your own choosing

Step 1: Put the flour, suet and salt into a bowl with a small amount of water and mix until you have a light dough. Roll this out on a lightly floured work surface into a thin (about 1cm thick) rectangle.
Step 2: Lavishly spread the jam all over the rectangle, leaving a margin of around 3cm around the edges.
Step 3: Roll the rectangle into a sausage shape. Wrap loosely in foil, allowing for the pudding to expand.
Step 4: Put water in the bottom of a steamer or fish kettle to below the metal rack and bring to the boil. Place the pudding on the rack and steam for around 2 hours, keeping the boiling water topped up throughout. Serve hot.

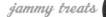 *jammy treats*

jammy bread and butter pudding

Bread and butter pudding is one of the best-loved desserts in Britain; one of the abiding 'school dinner' puddings that reminds us of childhood. In recent years, lots of chefs and restaurants have jazzed up this classic, using brioche or other speciality breads in the recipe. Spreading jam on the slices of bread gives you a lovely, fruity pudding, and serving it with homemade custard makes it even more like a 'school dinner'.

SERVES 4-6

8–10 slices of white bread
25g butter
150g jam of your choice
75g raisins
250ml whole milk
50ml cream
2 eggs
25g sugar

Step 1: Heat the oven to 200°C/gas mark 6.
Step 2: Cut the crusts off the bread and slice it into triangles. Butter the triangles and spread with jam. Carefully put them into a greased 25–30cm casserole dish, jam-side up, sprinkling the raisins between the layers of jammy slices. When you get to the top layer, it should be jam-side down.
Step 3: Warm the milk and cream in a pan. Whisk the eggs and sugar in a bowl and pour on the hot milk, whisking all the time, until the custard thickens.
Step 4: Pour the custard over the jammed-up bread and bake in the oven for about 40 minutes, until the pudding is golden on top.

queen of puddings

This old-fashioned and classic British pudding was supposedly invented for Queen Victoria, who was probably quite a large woman given how many puddings are named after her. It is a jammy cake mixture with a lovely, light meringue on top. You'll love it!

SERVES 4

400ml whole milk
100g white breadcrumbs
25g butter
75g sugar
4 eggs, separated
100g jam of your choice

Step 1: Heat the oven to 200°C/gas mark 6.

Step 2: Heat the milk in a pan over a low heat until it starts to bubble a little. Turn off the heat and add the breadcrumbs, butter and half the sugar. Leave to stand for about 15 minutes, then add the egg yolks.

Step 3: Put the mixture into a greased baking dish and bake in the oven for 30–35 minutes, or until golden brown.

Step 4: Meanwhile, whisk the egg whites and the rest of the sugar until you can turn the bowl upside down over your head (without getting any of the mixture on your head).

Step 5: Take the sponge out of the oven, spread the jam on top and spoon the meringue mixture over it.

Step 6: Put the pudding back into the oven for another 15 minutes or so, until the meringue is set and golden on top. Queen of Puddings is best served with a good helping of freshly made custard.

raspberry and cranberry cranachan

You may have picked up on the fact that I am from Scotland. In making SuperJam we use a lot of Scottish produce, and we have a great relationship with the local farmers, who do everything they can to make their fruit as tasty and natural as it can be. Cranachan is one of the most traditional of Scottish desserts, and, since it can be made using jam, I would be mad not to include it in the book. It is very simple and light and is often served on Burns Night, after a hearty feed of haggis, neeps and tatties.

MAKES 4–6 SERVINGS

50g rolled oats
150ml whipping cream
50g honey
50g Raspberry and Cranberry Jam
  (see page 30)
a measure of whisky
a handful of raspberries
mint leaf, to decorate (optional)

Step 1: Heat the oven to 150°C/gas mark 2. Spread the oats out on a baking tray and lightly toast them in the oven for 5–10 minutes. Be very careful not to burn them.
Step 2: Whip the cream until it is light and airy.
Step 3: Carefully fold the honey, jam and whisky into the cream, followed by the oats.
Step 4: Garnish with raspberries and some extra oats, and perhaps a mint leaf, if you want to be fancy.

jammy treats

bakewell tarts

The imaginatively named Bakewell Tart originates from the town of Bakewell. It is reputed that a cook in a local pub invented the pudding by mistake when he was trying to make jam tarts. A customer he served it to commented that it was 'baked well', and the name 'Bakewell' stuck, being a terribly witty pun on the name of the town. (This recipe tells you how to make individual tarts, but you can, of course, make one big tart using a 20cm-tart tin if you prefer.)

MAKES 6 MEDIUM TARTS

Pastry:
150g self-raising flour, plus extra for dusting
75g butter
25g sugar
1 egg, separated
a splash of milk

Filling:
200g jam of your choice
125g butter
125g sugar
3 eggs
125g ground almonds

Icing:
200g icing sugar
some glacé cherries

Step 1: Heat the oven to 180°C/gas mark 4.
Step 2: Rub the flour, butter and sugar together until you have breadcrumbs. You can use a food processor, if you have such gadgetry to hand.
Step 3: Add the yolk of the separated egg (keeping the white to one side) and a splash of milk, if needed, rubbing it together or blitzing it in the food processor until you have a nice dough.

jammy treats

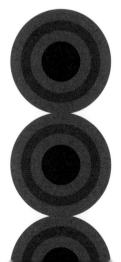

Step 4: If you have time, let the dough rest in the fridge for about 40 minutes, wrapped in clingfilm. Then roll it out on a floured surface until it is about 2cm thick and cut out circles, using a cutter (or the rim of a cup or glass if you don't have one).

Step 5: Put your pastry circles into individual greased loose-bottomed tart tins, 5–7cm in diameter. Prick the bottoms with a fork, glaze them lightly with the egg white, and proudly place them in the oven for about 20 minutes. Allow them to cool in the tins once they're done. Leave the oven on.

Step 6: Put a generous dollop of your chosen jam into each tart case and spread it out evenly. Mix the butter and sugar together, then beat the eggs in a bowl and gradually add them to the butter mixture. Stir in the ground almonds and spoon the mixture on top of the jam, leaving some space in the tarts for icing afterwards.

Step 7: Put the tarts back into the oven and bake for about 30 minutes, until the tops are golden brown. Take them out of the oven and let them cool. Once cool, carefully turn the tarts out of their tins. Mix the icing sugar with a little water, adding a few drops at a time until you have quite a thick icing. Spread the icing over the tops of the tarts and stick half a cherry on top.

jammy treats

steamed jam pudding

This is a lovely, simple pudding that is very comforting on a cold winter's evening. It is perfect served piping hot, with lots of custard.

SERVES 4-6

125g sugar
125g butter
½ lemon
4 eggs
250g self-raising flour
50ml whole milk
100g jam or curd of your choice

Step 1: Beat the sugar and butter together in a bowl, then add the zest of the lemon and gradually beat in the eggs, one at a time.
Step 2: Sift the flour onto the mixture and gently fold in, adding the milk until you have a soft but not runny mixture.
Step 3: Grease a large pudding basin (the sort you would use to make a Christmas pudding) or several small ones and put the jam in the bottom. Pour the cake mixture on top and cover the top tightly with foil.
Step 4: Put the bowl into a pan of boiling water, with the water reaching halfway up the sides of the bowl, and put a lid on top. Steam the pudding, topping up the water as needed, for the best part of 2 hours. Check that the pudding is ready by pressing the top of the sponge – it will be springy when it's done.
Step 5: Serve hot and with custard, if you like, along with a nice pot of tea.

arctic roll

Last year, I helped the celebrity chef Jason Atherton to make an Arctic Roll for the BBC's *The Great British Menu*, with the aim of jazzing up our favourite pudding. The Arctic Roll is certainly a British classic but has, sadly, been cheapened into a sickly sweet pudding for the kids and, like a lot of the puddings in this book, has gone out of fashion. This is a simplified version of the recipe Jason cooked on TV – a really luxurious pudding that is fun to serve to guests at a party.

MAKES 1 MEDIUM ROLL (SERVES 3–4)
150g caster sugar, plus extra to serve
150g butter
2 eggs
150g self-raising flour, sifted
a 400g tub of vanilla ice cream
(or homemade ice cream, see below)
a jam of your choosing

If you want to make your own ice-cream:
3 egg yolks
1 tablespoon caster sugar
250ml double cream
100ml whole milk
1 vanilla pod
50g jam if you want the ice cream
to be 'rippled'

To make the ice cream:
Step 1: Beat the egg yolks and sugar in a bowl until nice and creamy.
Step 2: Heat the cream, milk and vanilla until it is simmering. Remove the vanilla pod and add the hot cream to the egg yolks, whisking all the time. Put it all back into the pan on a low heat and cook for about 10 minutes, until it coats the back of a spoon. Strain the mixture through a sieve and leave to cool.
Step 3: Put the cooled mixture into your ice-cream machine. Or just put it into a tub in

 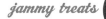

the freezer if you don't have such gadgetry and after a couple of hours, stir it and freeze some more. Do that a couple of times, until it starts to get thick and quite frozen.
Step 4: Now you can mix in the jam in swirls, if you're making it 'rippled', and put it all into the freezer overnight.

To make the sponge:
Step 5: Heat the oven to 200°C/gas mark 6.
Step 6: Whisk the sugar and butter together in a bowl until smooth. Whisk in the eggs and fold in the sifted flour, then spread the mixture out evenly on a shallow 25cm square baking tray. Place in the oven for about 10 minutes, or until the sponge is golden brown. Be extra careful not to overcook the sponge – you need it to remain quite soft so that you can wrap it around the ice cream.
Step 7: Allow the sponge to cool, then take it out of the tray and place it on top of a sheet of clingfilm or a tea towel bigger than the sponge. Spread the sponge with a generous layer of jam, then spoon the ice cream on top and roll the whole thing into a big sausage, so that the ice cream is wrapped all the way around with sponge. Pop it into the freezer for a few more hours, so that it becomes fairly solid. You can roll the Arctic Roll in sugar before serving it.

orange and passion fruit trifle

This trifle is made by layering slices of cake, whipped cream, custard and jam, curd or marmalade. I think it is perfect served with little amaretti biscuits, which you can either make using the recipe here or just buy ready-made if you don't have time.

SERVES 4-6

For the amaretti biscuits (makes about 12):
2 egg whites
100g sugar
50g ground almonds
a measure of Amaretto liqueur
a tablespoon of flaked almonds

For the cake:
100g sugar
100g butter
1 egg, beaten
100g self-raising flour

For the custard:
1 egg yolk
25g sugar
1 teaspoon cornflour
100ml cream or crème fraîche
¼ vanilla pod or 1 teaspoon vanilla essence

To finish the trifle:
300ml whipping cream
50g sugar
200g Orange and Passion Fruit Marmalade (see page 56)
4 passion fruits
1 orange

Step 1: To make the amaretti biscuits, first heat the oven to 180°C/gas mark 4. Beat the egg whites until light and fluffy, then fold in the sugar, ground almonds and Amaretto. Spoon onto a greased baking tray – the

jammy treats

dollops should be about the size of your thumb and spaced a few inches apart. Sprinkle the almonds on top and bake in the oven for about 20 minutes, or until golden. Step 2: For the cake, heat the oven to 200°C/ gas mark 6. Cream the sugar and butter together, mix in the egg and then fold in the flour. Pour into a reasonably deep greased cake tin, around 25cm in diameter, and bake in the oven for about 20 minutes. Step 3: Take the amaretti biscuits and the cake out of their tins and set aside to cool. For the custard, whip the egg yolk, sugar and cornflour together in a bowl. In a pan, heat the cream or crème fraiche with the vanilla until it starts bubbling. Pour the cream into the egg mixture, stirring all the time. Put it back into the pan and cook until it starts bubbling again. Set aside to cool and thicken. Step 4: Whip the cream and sugar together until the mixture forms 'peaks'. Cut the sponge cake into small rectangles or triangles, and place a layer in the bottom of 4–6 glasses. Spoon a layer of Orange and Passion Fruit Marmalade on top, then the custard and finally the whipped cream and sugar. Squeeze some passion fruit over the top of each and add a thin slice of orange to decorate. Step 5: Chill the trifles in the fridge for at least an hour before serving with the amaretti biscuits.

cheesecake

This recipe is for an 'unbaked' cheesecake, made with cream cheese and with a crushed biscuit base. It looks great if you put some fresh fruit on top or drizzle some jam over your cheesecake.

MAKES 1 LARGE CAKE FOR 4 PEOPLE, OR 4 INDIVIDUAL CAKES

150g digestive biscuits
75g butter
250g cream cheese
75g jam of your choice
50g icing sugar
75ml double cream

Step 1: Crush the digestive biscuits by placing them inside a clean tea towel and bashing it with a rolling pin until they are reduced to fine crumbs. Put them into a bowl. Melt the butter in a pan or in the microwave, then pour over the biscuits and mix well. Press the biscuit crumbs into the bottom of one large (25cm) loose-bottomed dish or 4 individual (7cm) dishes.

Step 2: Blend the cream cheese, jam and icing sugar with an electric whisk until very smooth. Now gradually blend in the cream until you have a smooth mixture.

Step 3: Spoon the mixture onto the biscuit base or bases and leave it to set in the fridge for at least 2 hours – ideally overnight.

New York cheesecake

New York cheesecake is similar to normal cheesecake but it is baked, which makes it more cake-like.

SERVES 6–8

150g digestive biscuits
50g butter
250g cream cheese
100g sugar
100g jam of your choice
50ml milk
2 eggs, beaten

Step 1: Heat the oven to 200°C/gas mark 6.
Step 2: Crush the digestive biscuits by placing them inside a clean tea towel and bashing it with a rolling pin until they are reduced to fine crumbs. Put them into a bowl. Melt the butter in the microwave or in a pan over a low heat and add it to the crushed biscuits. Mix well, then press the crumb mixture into a 25cm loose-bottomed or spring-release cake tin.
Step 3: Beat the cream cheese in a bowl until it is light and fluffy, then mix in the sugar, two-thirds of the jam and the milk. Add the eggs, mixing well after each one is added, then pour the mixture into the cake tin.
Step 4: Bake in the oven for 20 minutes or so, until the mixture has set and is slightly golden on top.
Step 5: Put the rest of the jam into a bowl and stir until it becomes a smooth sauce, adding a little water if needed. Drizzle it across the cheesecake in swirls or zig-zags, or whatever pattern you fancy.
Step 6: Chill the cheesecake in the fridge for a few hours before serving.

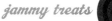

strawberry and white chocolate mousse with shortbread fingers

This mousse is really rich and creamy and is great if you make it with strawberry or blueberry jam. The little shortbread fingers are nice for dipping into the mousse. This is definitely a pudding to serve up to your chums at your next dinner party.

SERVES 6–8

For the shortbread fingers (makes 8–12):
100g butter
50g caster sugar
150g plain flour, sifted

For the mousse:
100g good-quality white chocolate
1 leaf of gelatine
250ml double cream
1 tablespoon caster sugar
100g strawberry jam, plus extra to serve
strawberries, to decorate (optional)

Step 1: Heat the oven to 200°C/gas mark 6.
Step 2: To make the shortbread fingers, beat the butter and sugar together until smooth and pale. Fold in the flour and continue to mix until you have a soft dough. Roll out the mixture on a lightly floured surface until it is 4cm thick and cut into fingers, or any other shape you like. Bake in the oven for 20 minutes or so, until firm and golden.
Step 3: Melt the chocolate in a bowl over a pan of boiling water (a 'bain marie') until it is smooth. The bowl must not touch the water.
Step 4: In a separate pan, mix the gelatine with 50ml of water. Once it has dissolved, add about 50ml of the cream and the sugar.

Stir over a medium heat until the mixture is simmering and the gelatine has dissolved.
Step 5: Add the gelatine mixture to the melted chocolate and whisk in the jam. In a separate bowl, whisk the rest of the cream, ideally with an electric whisk, until it starts to peak. Gradually fold the cream into the chocolate and jam mixture.
Step 6: Gently spoon the mixture into glasses to serve and refrigerate for at least a few hours. Serve topped with jam, or sliced strawberries, with the shortbread fingers alongside.

raspberry ripple
ice cream

Although raspberry is the usual candidate for being rippled through ice cream, you can use any kind of jam, curd or marmalade that you like. This recipe works best if you have an ice-cream machine, but don't worry if you haven't, you can make do without.

MAKES 1 LITRE OF ICE CREAM

6 eggs, separated
1 tablespoon caster sugar
500ml double cream
200ml whole milk
1 vanilla pod
200g Raspberry and Cranberry SuperJam (see page 30), or any jam, marmalade or curd of your choice

Step 1: Beat the egg yolks and sugar in a bowl until nice and creamy.

Step 2: Heat the cream, milk and vanilla until it is simmering. Remove the vanilla pod and add the hot cream to the egg yolks, whisking all the time. Put back into the pan on a low heat and cook for about 10 minutes, until it coats the back of a spoon. Strain the mixture and leave to cool.

Step 3: Put the cooled mixture into your ice-cream machine. Or put it into a plastic tub in the freezer if you don't have such gadgetry, and after a couple of hours, stir it and freeze some more. Do that a couple of times until it starts to get thick and quite frozen.

Step 4: Now you can mix in the jam in swirls and put it all into the freezer overnight.

jam tarts

These are very simple, and I think the way to make them most fun is to use a wide selection of fillings, so that your friends at the picnic or kids at the party can pick which one they fancy. It also looks a lot prettier when you have a whole selection of colours.

MAKES 8–12 LITTLE TARTS
200g self-raising flour, plus extra for dusting
a pinch of salt
100g butter
1 egg yolk
75g caster sugar
a jar of jam (or jams!) of your choosing

Step 1: Sift the flour into a bowl, add the salt, then rub in the butter with your fingers until you have a nice crumbly mixture.
Step 2: Mix in the egg yolk and caster sugar with a wooden spoon until you have a dough – add occasional splashes of water, as needed, until the dough is well combined.
Step 3: Put the dough into the fridge for about 15 minutes and heat the oven to 200°C/gas mark 6 in the meantime.
Step 4: Roll the dough out on a lightly floured surface and cut out little circles. Put them into lightly greased tart tins and prick them in a few places with a fork.
Step 5: Put a generous blob of jam into the tarts, so they are about three-quarters full. You can use any kind of jam you fancy, and it is probably nicest to use a few different kinds.
Step 6: Roll out the leftover dough and cut out little stars or any other shapes you fancy. Place these on top of the jam. Put your little beauties into the oven for about 20 minutes, until the pastry is golden and the jam is bubbling hot. Let them cool on a wire rack before you get stuck in.

banoffee cupcakes

Cupcakes have become something of a craze in recent years, with celebrities in Hollywood apparently eating them all the time. There are cupcake shops popping up all over the place, selling weird and wonderful cupcakes in all shapes and sizes. These banoffee cupcakes are my contribution to the movement, filled with Banana and Rum curd and toffee fondant. Mmm!

MAKES 10 MEDIUM CUPCAKES

Cake mix:
100g butter or margarine
100g sugar
2 eggs, beaten
100g self-raising flour

Toffee fondant:
50g butter
50g brown sugar
50ml whole milk
100g icing sugar

Filling:
100g Banana and Rum curd (see page 72)

Step 1: Heat the oven to 200°C/gas mark 6.
Step 2: Beat the butter and sugar together until smooth, then mix in the eggs.
Step 3: Sift the flour onto the mixture and gently fold in. Spoon the mixture into 10–12 standard paper baking cases.
Step 4: Bake in the oven for about 20–25 minutes, or until the cakes have risen and are golden. Allow them to cool on a wire rack.
Step 5: Meanwhile, make the toffee fondant. Melt the butter in a pan and stir in the brown sugar until dissolved. Add the milk and bring to a rolling boil. Put the icing sugar in a bowl and add the hot butter mixture, mixing thoroughly until you have a smooth toffee.
Step 6: Using a teaspoon, carefully remove the centre of each cupcake. Spoon a little of the toffee fondant into the hole then a little of the banana and rum curd on top.

jammy treats

viennese swirls

These are great little Scottish biscuits (I've no idea why they are called Viennese) and are one of my personal favourites; the biscuit is light and crumbly and I could eat quite a few of them at once. As with the jam tarts, it's a nice idea to use a selection of fillings.

MAKES 8 SMALL BISCUITS
For the biscuits:
30g icing sugar
100g butter
1 teaspoon vanilla essence
150g flour, sifted

For the filling:
50g butter
50g icing sugar, plus extra for dusting
dash of vanilla essence
a jam of your choosing

Step 1: Heat the oven to 180°C/gas mark 4.
Step 2: With a wooden spoon, mix the icing sugar, butter and vanilla essence together until you have a nice smooth paste. Add the flour and mix until you have a fairly solid dough.
Step 3: Using an icing bag, pipe the dough in swirls onto a greased baking tray and bake them for about 10–12 minutes, or until they are golden brown.
Step 4: Allow the swirls to cool on a wire rack. In the meantime, prepare a vanilla fondant by beating the icing sugar and butter together with a dash of vanilla essence.
Step 5: Spread half the swirls with the jam and then sandwich them together with the other half using the fondant. You can give them a little sprinkle with icing sugar afterwards, which makes them look even better.

 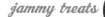

macarons

Macarons are extremely popular in France and come in all kinds of colours, flavours and sizes. They are quite expensive to buy in bakeries, since they are very fiddly to make and quite often batches don't work out. You definitely need to be willing to make a few attempts and have a little patience – but, I promise you, it will all be worth it because macarons are very pretty and taste amazing.

MAKES ABOUT 6 MEDIUM MACARONS

4 egg whites
100g ground almonds
200g caster sugar
a pinch of salt
food colouring (optional)
50g jam of your choice
50g butter
50g icing sugar

Step 1: Heat the oven to 150°C/gas mark 2.
Step 2: Beat the egg whites until they are fluffy and stiff enough for you to be able to turn the bowl upside down – ideally use an electric whisk, otherwise it'll take you a long time. Macarons are basically a form of meringue, so you need the egg whites to be whisked for ages, until you can make 'peaks' with the whisk.
Step 3: In a separate bowl, combine the ground almonds with 50g of the caster sugar.
Step 4: Add a pinch of salt to the egg whites and then add the rest of the sugar 1 teaspoon at a time, beating continuously. It is important to add it gradually, even though it takes a while, so that the mixture stays light and fluffy and doesn't go runny. If you want the macarons to be colourful, which you probably do, this is the point at which you should add a drop of colouring.
Step 5: Now you can gradually add the almond

mixture, folding it in one spoon at a time.
Step 6: Draw circles on some baking paper, in the size that you want your macarons to be. Put all the mixture into a piping bag and pipe it into the circles. Bake in the oven for about 20 minutes, or until the macarons are firm. Step 7: Combine the jam, butter and icing sugar in a bowl until you have a smooth buttercream that you can use to stick the macarons together in pairs. You could use Lemon curd (see page 69) or Homemade Pistachio Butter (see page 98) too.

jammy dodgers

These are very easy to make and are particularly fun for kids to help with. Instead of the jam you can try substituting chocolate spread (see page 91) and adding cocoa to the recipe, if you fancy.

MAKES ABOUT 12 BISCUITS

100g sugar
200g butter
100g plain flour, plus extra for dusting
100g jam or curd of your choice

Step 1: Heat the oven to 200°C/gas mark 6.
Step 2: Beat the sugar and butter together until light and smooth. Sift in the flour and mix until you have a stiff dough.
Step 3: Roll the dough out on a floured surface and cut out hearts, using a cutter. Cut little heart-shaped windows in the middle of half of them (or you can just cut a circle if you prefer). Pop them onto a greased baking tray and bake for about 15 minutes, or until golden brown round the edges.
Step 4: Sandwich your little hearts together with jam, curd or chocolate spread and sprinkle generously with icing sugar.

peanut butter *cookies*

If you've been making your own peanut butter (see page 90), you're probably looking for something to do with it. These cookies are quite addictive and usually won't last long once they've come out of the oven. You can also try adding chocolate chips to the recipe, or replacing the peanut butter with pistachio butter (see page 98).

MAKES ABOUT 12 COOKIES

100g sugar
75g butter
100g peanut butter
1 egg, beaten
150g self-raising flour

Step 1: Heat the oven to 200°C/gas mark 6.
Step 2: Beat the sugar and butter until light and smooth, then mix in the peanut butter and the egg. Sift in the flour and mix until you have a stiff dough.
Step 3: Roll the dough out on a floured surface and cut out circles, using a cutter about 10cm in diameter. Pop them onto a greased baking tray and bake in the oven for about 15 minutes, or until golden brown round the edges.

muffins

These American-style muffins, filled with jam, are delicious. I suggest using Blueberry and Blackcurrant SuperJam (see page 29) for a juicy, jammy twist on a classic blueberry muffin.

(see page 29)

MAKES ABOUT 6 BIG MUFFINS

60g sugar
100g butter
2 eggs, beaten
100g plain flour
1 teaspoon baking powder
100g jam of your choice

Step 1: Heat the oven to 200°C/gas mark 6.
Step 2: Beat the sugar and butter together until you have a smooth paste. Gradually add the eggs, beating all the time. Add the flour and baking powder and continue to mix well.
Step 3: Fill the muffin cases halfway up with the mixture and add a teaspoonful of jam, making sure it is in the middle so that it won't ooze out of the sides of the muffin. Pour the rest of the mixture on top.
Step 4: Bake the muffins in the oven for about 20 minutes, or until golden. You might like to serve them with cream as soon as they come out of the oven.

financiers

These traditional French teacakes are made using special boat-shaped baking tins. If you don't have any, you can use regular individual muffin tins.

MAKES 8–10 SMALL FINANCIERS

50g ground almonds
100g butter
30g plain flour
100g icing sugar
a pinch of salt
3 egg whites
1 teaspoon vanilla extract
50g jam of your choice

Step 1: Heat the oven to 200°C/gas mark 6.
Step 2: Put the ground almonds on a baking tray and lightly brown them in the oven for 5–10 minutes. Remove from the oven, but leave it on.
Step 3: Heat the butter in a pan until it looks clear and the milk solids have darkened at the bottom of the pan. Strain through a sieve or muslin and let it cool down. This is called a 'beurre noisette'. Use a little of it to grease the baking tins.
Step 4: Whisk together the ground almonds, flour, icing sugar and salt. In a separate bowl, whisk the egg whites and fold into the mixture, along with the vanilla and the melted butter.
Step 5: Pour the mixture into the greased tins, then put them into the oven and bake for 5 minutes. Take them out and make a little groove in the middle of each one by pressing your thumb down into them about 1.5cm deep. Put a teaspoonful of jam into each groove, then pop them back into the oven and bake for 5–10 minutes, until golden brown.

 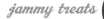

jam doughnuts

Making your own fresh doughnuts is a lot of fun, and I guarantee that the end result is unlike any doughnut you'll be able to buy ready-made. Fill them with jam and custard and eat them when they're still hot.

MAKES 6 DOUGHNUTS

175g bread flour, sifted
75ml water
20g butter
10g yeast
a pinch of salt
400ml vegetable oil
200g jam of your choice
50g caster sugar

Step 1: With a wooden spoon, mix the flour, water, butter, yeast and salt in a bowl until you have a dough – this will take a good few minutes of mixing.
Step 2: Cover the bowl with a damp towel and leave the dough to rise for about 30 minutes.
Step 3: Roll the dough into small balls, about the size of a ping-pong ball, and let them rise on their own for another 30 minutes or so, in a bowl or on a tray, covered with a damp towel.
Step 4: Heat the oil in a large pan or deep-fat fryer until it starts bubbling. Fry the balls in small batches for 5–10 minutes, until they are golden. Drain them on kitchen paper – that way you avoid them being too greasy.
Step 5: Using a large syringe or piping bag with a narrow, sharp nozzle, inject the doughnuts with jam. You can also inject some custard or cream if you want to push the boat out. Roll the doughnuts in caster sugar and eat them right away!

scones

At the SuperJam tea parties we go through literally tens of thousands of scones! We never seem to have enough at each event, with everyone eating several by the end of the afternoon. Traditionally, scones are served with clotted cream. There is a long-running dispute about whether to put the jam or the cream on top. In Devon, they say you should put the jam on top of the cream, in Cornwall they put the cream on top of the jam.

MAKES 8–12 MEDIUM SCONES
250g self-raising flour, plus extra for dusting
a pinch of salt
75g butter
30g caster sugar
150ml milk
jam or curd of your choice, to serve

Step 1: Heat the oven to 200°C/gas mark 6.
Step 2: Sift the flour into a bowl, add the salt, and then, with your fingers, rub in the butter.
Step 3: Stir in the sugar, add some of the milk and mix it with your fingers. Keep adding the milk in stages until you have a lovely dough that doesn't stick to your fingers any more.
Step 4: Give the dough a wee knead on a floury surface, then break off clumps by hand (you could flatten it out and cut out pretty little circles with a cutter, if you're a bit fancy) and pop them onto a greased baking tray.
Step 5: Brush your little creations with a dash of milk and set them on their merry way for a 15-minute baking, until they've risen up and look nice and golden.

apple and cinnamon scones

These scones have a lovely festive spiciness and are great served with Blueberry and Blackcurrant SuperJam (see page 29) and clotted cream. You could try using pears in place of the apples if you want to try something a bit different.

MAKES 8–12 MEDIUM SCONES
250g self-raising flour
a pinch of salt
1 teaspoon ground cinnamon
75g butter
1 cooking apple
30g brown sugar
150ml milk

Step 1: Heat the oven to 200°C/gas mark 6.
Step 2: Sift the flour into a bowl, add the salt and cinnamon, and then, with your fingers, rub in the butter. Peel, core and finely grate the apple and stir it into the buttery flour.
Step 3: Stir in the sugar, then add a little milk and mix it in with your fingers. Keep adding the milk in stages until you have a lovely dough that doesn't stick to your fingers any more.
Step 4: Give the dough a wee knead on a floury surface, then break off clumps by hand (you could flatten it out and cut out pretty little circles with a cutter, if you're that way inclined) and pop them on to a greased baking tray.
Step 5: Brush your little creations with a dash of milk and set them on their merry way for a 15-minute baking, until they've risen up and look nice and golden.

treacle *scones*

These scones are my favourite and are quite traditional in Scotland. Treacle is similar to molasses, which you could use instead if you're reading my book in a faraway land that doesn't sell treacle. They have a lovely brown colour and aren't awfully sweet, which you might imagine they would be.

MAKES 8–12 MEDIUM SCONES

250g self-raising flour
a pinch of salt
1 teaspoon ground cinnamon (optional)
75g butter
30g caster sugar
2 tablespoons black treacle
150ml milk

Step 1: Heat the oven to 200°C/gas mark 6.
Step 2: Sift the flour into a bowl, add the salt and cinnamon, if using, and then, with your fingers, rub in the butter.
Step 3: Stir in the sugar and treacle, then add some milk and mix it in with your fingers. Keep adding the milk in stages until you have a lovely dough that doesn't stick to your fingers any more.
Step 4: Give the dough a wee knead on a floury surface, then break off clumps by hand (you could flatten it out and cut out pretty little circles with a cutter, if you're that way inclined) and pop them on a greased baking tray.
Step 5: Brush your little creations with a dash of milk and set them on their merry way for a 15-minute baking, until they've risen up and look nice and golden.

blueberry and
blackcurrant oat slices

These simple bars are quite similar to flapjacks but they have a nice gooey layer of Blueberry and Blackcurrant SuperJam in the middle.

MAKES ABOUT 6 SLICES

75g brown sugar
125g self-raising flour
200g rolled oats
100g butter
150g Blueberry and Blackcurrant SuperJam (see page 29) or any jam of your choice

Step 1: Heat the oven to 200°C/gas mark 6.
Step 2: Mix the sugar, flour and oats in a bowl, and rub in the butter using your fingers until you've got a nice dough.
Step 3: Grease a medium sized baking tin, about 25cm long, then divide the dough in half and roll each half to about 1cm thick – it should be about the same size and shape as the tin. Place one half in the tin, spread the jam on top and lay the rest of the dough on top of the jam. Bake in the oven for about 25 minutes, or until the oats have turned golden brown. Cut it into slices once it's all cooled.

millefeuille

In French 'mille feuilles' means 'a thousand leaves'. Traditionally a millefeuille is made with several layers of puff pastry, sandwiched with confectioner's custard and, very often, with jam. It is sometimes called 'vanilla slice' or 'custard slice' in Britain, and in America it is known as a 'Napoleon'.

SERVES 3

100g flour, plus extra for dusting
400g sugar
12 egg yolks
750ml whole milk
1 vanilla pod
200g puff pastry
100g jam of your choice
icing sugar, to dust

Step 1: Whisk the flour, sugar and egg yolks in a bowl until very light. Meanwhile, bring the milk to the boil in a pan with the vanilla pod.
Step 2: Remove the vanilla pod and whisk the hot milk into the fluffy egg mix, then return the mixture to the pan and gradually bring to the boil, stirring constantly. Pour into a bowl and pop it into the fridge for 40 minutes or so.
Step 3: Heat the oven to 200°C/gas mark 6.
Step 4: Roll out the puff pastry thinly on a lightly floured surface. Place it on a greased baking tray and bake for 15 minutes, or until it has puffed up. Allow the pastry to cool on a wire rack, then cut into 3 long rectangles or 9 small rectangles, using a very sharp knife.
Step 5: Take the milk mixture out of the fridge and give it a good whisk.
Step 6: Spread jam carefully onto one of the pastry slices, and put a generous layer of the now quite firm milk mix on top. Lay the next pastry slice on top and repeat the layers. Put the final slice of pastry on top, and give it a dusting with icing sugar.

linzer bars

The Linzertorte is a traditional Austrian tart which actually claims to be the oldest tart in the world. It is filled with jam or compote and topped with pastry in a lattice style. These bars are a simple version of the Linzertorte and are great filled with any kind of jam, but Cherries and Berries or Blueberry and Blackcurrant SuperJam (see pages 47, 29) work particularly well.

(see pages 47, 29)

MAKES ABOUT 12 BARS

175g sugar
200g butter
1 egg, beaten
1 lemon
400g plain flour
1 teaspoon ground cinnamon
100g ground almonds
150g jam of your choice
icing sugar, to dust

Step 1: Heat the oven to 200°C/gas mark 6.

Step 2: Beat the sugar and butter together until they're nice and smooth. Add the egg, along with the zest and juice of the lemon, and mix a bit more. Now mix in the flour, cinnamon and ground almonds and give it a good beating until you have a reasonably stiff dough.

Step 3: Press half the dough over the bottom of a greased rectangular cake tin, around 20cm in length, and spread all the jam on top. Roll out the rest of the dough nice and flat and cut it into strips. Place the strips in a lattice on top of the jam, letting some jam peek through the gaps.

Step 4: Bake in the oven for 20 minutes or so, until slightly golden on top.

Step 5: Take the tart out of the oven, remove from the tin and cool on a wire rack. When cool, sprinkle with the icing sugar and cut into bars.

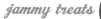

almond and jam meringue bars

These little bars have an almondy base with meringue on top and a layer of jam in between.

MAKES ABOUT 10 BARS

200g butter
150g ground almonds
100g brown sugar
4 eggs
250g plain flour, sifted
170g caster sugar
200g jam of your choice
50g desiccated coconut

Step 1: Heat the oven to 200°C/gas mark 6.
Step 2: With a wooden spoon, cream together the butter, almonds and brown sugar. Beat one of the eggs and stir it in, then add the flour gradually until you have a smooth mixture.
Step 3: Spread the mixture evenly in a greased 30cm baking tray and bake for about 15 minutes, or until golden brown.
Step 4: Separate the 3 remaining eggs and put the whites into a bowl (you do not need the yolks for this recipe). Add the caster sugar and whisk until the mixture is light and fluffy and you could hold the bowl upside down above your head, if you wanted to. This will take 10–15 minutes. Take the almond base out of the oven and generously spread the top with the jam. Reduce the oven temperature to 150°C/gas mark 2.
Step 5: Spread the meringue over the jam, sprinkle the coconut on top and put back into the oven for another 15–20 minutes, until the meringue is golden on top. Remove from the tin and cool on a wire rack then cut into bars.

victoria sponge

As the name suggests, this simple cake was named after a lady called Victoria; in this case it was Queen Victoria. The great thing about it is that you can fill it with whatever you like: jam, curd, cream or fresh fruit. You can even make it with several layers.

MAKES 6 LARGE SLICES

200g butter or margarine
200g sugar
4 eggs, beaten
200g self-raising flour
100g jam or curd of your choice
icing sugar, to dust

Step 1: Heat the oven to 200°C/gas mark 6.
Step 2: Beat the butter and sugar together until smooth, then stir in the beaten eggs.
Step 3: Sift the flour onto the mixture and gently fold in until well combined. Spoon the mixture into 2 greased baking tins, about 20cm in diameter.
Step 4: Bake in the oven for 20 minutes, or until the cakes have risen and are golden on top.
Step 5: Remove the sponge cakes from their trays and leave them to cool on a wire rack. Sandwich them together with jam or curd, and dust the top with icing sugar.

jammy treats

battenberg cake

Battenberg cake is made so that it has a distinctive checked pattern when you cut it in half, and this homemade version is great, especially if you go to the extra effort of making your own marzipan to wrap around the cake.

MAKES 1 CAKE

125g self-raising flour
125g butter
125g sugar
3 eggs, beaten
1 teaspoon vanilla extract
2 tablespoons milk
1 drop of red colouring
75g jam (apricot works well)
200g marzipan, homemade (see below)
    or bought

To make your own marzipan:
75g icing sugar
1 egg
150g ground almonds

Step 1: Heat the oven to 180°C/gas mark 4.
Step 2: To make the cake, beat together the flour, butter, sugar, eggs, vanilla and milk until smooth. Divide the mixture between 2 bowls; add a drop of red colouring (or another colour if you feel like it) to one bowl and mix. You can add a different colour to each mixture if you like, or leave one plain, which is traditional. Bake the mixes in 2 separate rectangular loaf tins (20cm long) lined with baking paper, for 20–30 minutes, until golden . Set aside to cool on a wire rack.
Step 3: While the cakes are baking, you can make the marzipan if you are going to make your own. Whisk the sugar and egg in a bowl

over a pan of simmering water for about 10 minutes, until it is thick. Remove from the heat and stir in the ground almonds, until you have a smooth dough. Let the mixture chill in the fridge for about half an hour and, hey presto, you have marzipan!

Step 4: When the cakes have cooled down, trim them so that you have 4 long bricks of cake, 2 in each colour. Generously coat all the pieces with jam and arrange them 2 across, 2 up, in alternate colours.

Step 5: Roll out the marzipan into a sheet 1cm thick and carefully wrap around the cake, covering all the sides.

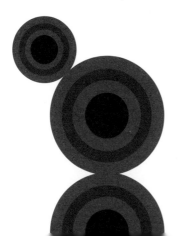

rice pudding

Rice pudding is probably the simplest pudding in this book; it doesn't take many ingredients and you probably have them all in your cupboard and fridge right now. It is definitely a classic and a great comfort food; you'll love it with a big dollop of your homemade jam!

SERVES 4–6

1 litre whole milk
200g short-grain rice
100g sugar
1 teaspoon vanilla extract or 1 vanilla pod
50g raisins
½ teaspoon grated nutmeg
200g jam of your choice

Step 1: Put the milk and rice into a pan over a low heat and simmer for about 25 minutes, until the rice is cooked. Make sure you stir the mixture regularly, so that the rice doesn't stick to the bottom of the pan.
Step 2: Add the sugar, vanilla, raisins and nutmeg and cook for another 10 minutes, until the mixture is nice and thick.
Step 3: Remove the vanilla pod, if using, and pour the mixture into serving bowls – you can eat it hot or cold. Serve with a generous blob of whatever jam you like.

swiss roll

It's funny how names came about in the olden days. A Swiss roll never came from Switzerland; it most probably originated from Germany. In Venezuela they called the same pudding 'Gypsy Arm', which I thought was a funnier name for it. As with a lot of the puddings in this book, you can use any kind of jam or curd you like for the filling. You could even add cocoa powder to the cake mixture and use whipped cream in the filling, as well as the jam.

SERVES 3-4

4 eggs
100g sugar
100g self-raising flour
50g icing sugar, plus extra to dust
50g butter, softened
100g jam of your choice

Step 1: Heat the oven to 200°C/gas mark 6.
Step 2: Whisk the eggs and sugar until they are firm enough for you to be able to hold the bowl above your head without them dropping out. Fold in the flour until it is well mixed, then spread the mixture evenly in a rectangle on a greased, shallow 25cm baking tray and pop it into the oven for 15 minutes, until golden.
Step 3: Remove the sponge from the baking tray and lay it on a clean tea towel. Roll it up into a sausage shape, using the towel to help you, then set it aside and leave it to cool in the towel. In the meantime, whisk the icing sugar and butter together to make buttercream.
Step 4: Unroll the sponge and trim the edges with a sharp knife, so that it looks nice and neat. Put it back on the tea towel and generously spread it with the buttercream, followed by the jam. Gently roll up the sponge until you have a big sausage, then remove the tea towel and sprinkle the whole thing with icing sugar.

jammy treats

index

index

Writing this book has been a lot of fun and all of my friends and family have been happy to try out all of the cakes and puddings I've been making recently!

I want to take the opportunity to thank Imogen Fortes at Ebury for making *The SuperJam Cookbook* happen; Noel Murphy for taking such amazing photographs; and Smith & Gilmour for designing the book so beautifully. Thanks also to my agent Jonathan Conway at Mulcahy Conway Associates.

Nothing I've done over the past few years could have happened if my loving parents, Anne and Robert, and brother Connor hadn't helped me along the way and let me use their kitchen for years. Mum, Dad and Connor; thank you for supporting me on my jam adventure!